CIGAR

To Gary & Julye —
Best wishes.

[signature] 10/25/96

CIGAR
AMERICA'S HORSE

JAY HOVDEY

THE BLOOD-HORSE, INC.
LEXINGTON, KENTUCKY

ISBN 0-939049-79-1

PRINTED IN THE UNITED STATES OF AMERICA
FIRST EDITION: OCTOBER 1996
1 2 3 4 5 6 7 8 9 10

This book is dedicated to

Edward William Hovdey and Brady Thomas Mott,

champions among young men.

"If personality is an unbroken series of successful gestures, then there was something gorgeous about him, some heightened sensitivity to the promises of life, as if he were related to one of those intricate machines that register earthquakes ten thousand miles away."

— F. SCOTT FITZGERALD,
"THE GREAT GATSBY"

CONTENTS

Introduction 1

Nativity 5

Airborne 27

Frustration 49

Heartland 69

Awakening 89

Control 105

Perfection 123

Summit 147

Armageddon 163

Streak 181

Epilogue..205

About the Author 208

Cigar's Past Performances 209

Pedigree/Family Notes 210

Acknowledgments 212

A 24-page photo section appears after page 118

INTRODUCTION

Persistent storm clouds had passed during the night, and now the early morning sun was pounding down, promising a blazing day in the desert. A puff of wind stirred the fine sand covering the stable grounds and lifted the light, cotton mesh blanket draped over the big horse in the middle of the yard. He was standing stone still—a dark brown statue with an unruly black mane and a white emblem the shape of South America stamped between the eyes.

Nearby, their long shadows trickling across the khaki-colored sand, four people talked among themselves in hushed tones reserved for church. They could have been screaming for all it mattered. The big horse was oblivious to their presence. He faced the breeze, lowered his head, and let the lids of his eyes creep slowly downward. It was hot. He was tired.

He had a right. Barely twelve hours had passed since the big horse named Cigar had run the race of a lifetime to defeat fellow American Soul of the Matter in the deep, tiring sand of Nad Al Sheba racetrack. The experience had taken its toll. In a professional career that had spanned three years and twenty-seven races, Cigar had never been so exhausted. There was a small swelling in his left front ankle. His appetite was dull. If he could have talked he would have said without hesitation, "Take me home. Now."

Home was back in New York, but the big horse had become a citizen of the world. Nad Al Sheba was located in the sheikhdom of Dubai, one of the seven United Arab

Emirates lining the southernmost coast of the Persian Gulf. Cigar had journeyed half a world away from the familiar sights and smells of the American racing scene. He had done what no champion American thoroughbred ever had done before. Defying both precedent and logic, scorning his own physical frailties, Cigar had left the safe haven of the United States to travel seven thousand miles and defeat an all-star international field in the Dubai World Cup, winning a prize of $2.4 million and a permanent place in history.

True believers in Cigar had come to expect nothing less. The Dubai World Cup, contested on March 27, 1996, was Cigar's fourteenth consecutive victory, dating back to October of 1994. Cigar already was the reigning American Horse of the Year. During the 1995 season, Cigar had won all ten of his races, a feat matched only once in the past sixty years. He had appeared in Florida, Arkansas, Maryland, Massachusetts, California and New York, facing the best the competition could muster from the talent pool of recent thoroughbred generations. Through it all, Cigar could not be beaten. Cigar would not be beaten.

But Dubai was different. Dubai raised the historical stakes. This was Muhammad Ali decking George Foreman in Zaire, Greg LeMond cycling to his third Tour de France, the American ice hockey team taking the gold in Lake Placid. Victory in Dubai set Cigar apart from the great American thoroughbreds to which he had been relentlessly compared. There was no Dubai for Secretariat or Seattle Slew. No Dubai for Affirmed. And no Dubai for Spectacular Bid. They had earned their greatness through traditional means, through traditional American events.

Cigar did all that…and then he added Dubai.

In truth, there was nothing traditional about Cigar, nor in the path he took to greatness. He was not some adolescent tennis phenom or a teenage basketball bonus baby going pro after one year of college. Cigar was a hardened equine adult by the time his true nature flourished, despite the fact that he was provided with the blood of champions and all the advantages of a proper upbringing by Allen and Madeleine Paulson, the people who bred him and raced him. Cigar had the benefit of excellent schooling from the moment he saw a bridle. He was trained at the track by two men who knew how to handle champions. But he drove them all to distraction. Cigar was nothing more than a frustrating tease at age three and an abject failure for most of his four-year-old season. He was, quite literally, the last of his class to graduate.

Then, on that watershed day in October of '94, Cigar began winning races as if his life depended upon the outcome. After his sixth straight win at Oaklawn Park in Hot Springs, Arkansas, skeptics ran for cover. After his ninth straight win in the Hollywood Gold Cup in Los Angeles, fans began chanting his name. After his twelfth straight win in the Breeders' Cup Classic at Belmont Park in October of 1995, Cigar had transcended the parochial boundaries of thoroughbred racing and had become a bona fide sports superstar.

On went Cigar's winning streak, deep into his 1996 campaign, as he chased the elusive sixteen straight set so long ago by Citation. With each thrilling victory more and more fans fell under his spell, until anyone who had heard of the sport at least knew the name of Cigar. They lined the pathways and hung from the grandstands in Boston, some twenty-two thousand strong. Local politicians knew a good crowd when they saw one and took notes. In Chicago, where the streak finally reached sweet sixteen, Cigar was treated like a rock star by the thirty-four thousand on hand and cheered as if he were playing for the hometown Bulls. When the streak ended at Del Mar, before a record throng of forty-four thousand and change, Cigar was saluted in rare defeat as if he had carried the day.

Still, Cigar remained an enigma, inscrutable even in the face of a drama as public as the Citation chase or the Dubai World Cup. As he dozed that morning in the desert sun, getting his last few whiffs of an Arabian spring before heading home to New York and the remainder of the historic '96 campaign, he appeared to be just another well-made horse, bearing a landscape of battle scars earned from his years of training and racing. It was in motion that he became something else—fierce, efficient and unforgiving. Madeleine Paulson, standing near Cigar that morning with his trainer, Bill Mott, said quietly, almost to herself, "I wonder now if people will realize just how great he is?"

This is the story of that greatness. This is the story of Cigar.

CHAPTER 1

NATIVITY

The cars came skidding into the lot at the Red Mile trotting track and parked wherever they could. People piled out, wrapped in jackets against the early spring chill, and dashed headlong for the doors. They were running late. It was almost post time. Inside, a crowd of more than a thousand already had packed themselves thick as Iowa cornstalks around the banks of video monitors. It was ten o'clock in the morning in Lexington, the heart of Kentucky horse country. And up there on the television screens, flickering in muted color, was a scene straight out of a dream. Live from the other side of the world, America's horse was about to perform.

Ted Carr, easy to spot beneath his weather-beaten Brookside Farm cap, had a good view staked out near one of the screens. He was nervous. He didn't know what to expect. It was tough enough watching the big horse from afar when he ran in Florida, or California, or New York. At least Carr knew what it took to win in places like that. He had been breeding and raising thoroughbreds his whole life just so they could be good enough to compete at the top of the game. But this Dubai race was something different. The idea was unbelievable, and the circumstances were downright daunting, even for the big horse. Even for Cigar.

A few minutes later, as Cigar caught sight of Soul of the

Matter making his move on the outside, Carr was beating on bystanders and screaming like a wounded bear. Around him the crowd rattled the rafters with their cheers as Soul of the Matter drew even with Cigar, then bobbed his nose in front. "Most horses, that happens to them when they're tired, they are done," Carr said later. But in the heat of the moment, his eyes never flinched from the television. The sixty-one-year-old hardboot went to riding, whipping and driving in rhythm with Jerry Bailey's every move aboard Cigar. Up on the screen, Cigar thrust his head back in front and slowly began to squeeze the last ounce of challenge out of the gallant Soul of the Matter. Then it was over, and Cigar had won. Ted Carr's baby had won.

Carr was overwhelmed with pride. Friends pounded him on the back as if he had been right there in the saddle with Bailey. He brushed away a shameless tear and let his mind wander back to the spirited little foal the farm hands called The Hammer. As soon as he could, Carr phoned his son, Mac, back at Brookside with the news. It was Mac who had given Cigar his early lessons. And it was Mac who had nursed Cigar through an injury that could have ended the story before it began.

The beginning. Cigar had several. Pedigree experts will take you on a tour of a family tree that spreads from Canada to Argentina, and before that to England and France. Cigar's contemporary history got its real start on the afternoon of July 19, 1982, at the prestigious Keeneland July yearling sale, where Nelson Bunker Hunt, on the urging of partner Bruce McNall, bid $130,000 to buy a chestnut colt by The Minstrel, one of Northern Dancer's finest sons. Later, Hunt named him Palace Music and sent him to train in France. The next moment of significance on Cigar's time line occurred March 19, 1984, at Hollywood Park, when Rick Bracken, Allen Paulson's California farm manager, spent $510,000 of Paulson's money to buy a daughter of Triple Crown winner Seattle Slew named Solar Slew. It was the highest price paid anywhere for a two-year-old filly that year.

Palace Music, long-necked and leggy, did not race until he was three. Still, he was among the best of his generation. He was imposing and powerful, with a bright copper coat and a broad white blaze that spilled down over his nostrils and chin. Midway through 1984, Paulson bought half of Palace Music in a package with several other horses owned by Hunt and McNall. The colt ended his first year of competition with a victory over the champion filly Pebbles in the Dubai Champion Stakes at Newmarket.

Solar Slew, on the other hand, was a flop, despite the fact that she was trained in California by Ron McAnally. Through the early 1980s, the McAnally stable was the most famous address in American racing as the home of John Henry. By 1984, John Henry was a nine-year-old legend who was on his way to more than $6.5-million in earnings and his second Horse of the Year title. Solar Slew never met John Henry, but she may have caught a glimpse of Palace Music, her future mate, late in 1985 when he was briefly stabled with McAnally.

"It was a mistake," recalled Eduardo Inda, McAnally's assistant trainer at the time. "They brought in this beautiful chestnut and put him in our barn. I guess it was because we had a lot of horses for Mr. Paulson. But he was supposed to go to Charlie Whittingham. A couple weeks later they came and got him. Too bad for us."

Too bad indeed. Palace Music was one of the best grass horses in North America in 1986. His most important win was, fittingly, the John Henry Handicap at Hollywood Park. But his finest hour came in the Breeders' Cup Mile at Santa Anita when he finished second to the French longshot Last Tycoon. Palace Music began his stallion career in 1987 with double duty, breeding in the spring at Nelson Bunker Hunt's Bluegrass Farm in Lexington and then in New Zealand during the fall. When he returned to America for the 1988 breeding season he was relocated to Brookside Farm.

Laura de Seroux knew Palace Music as well as anyone on earth. As an advisor to the racing program of Hunt and McNall, and a professional exercise rider as well, she literally followed the horse back and forth between Europe and America. And, as the wife of Allen Paulson's bloodstock manager, Emmanuel de Seroux, she enjoyed a unique perspective when it came to analyzing the imprint of Palace Music upon his most famous son, Cigar.

"Palace was wonderful to gallop," Laura de Seroux said. "He gave you a wonderful feeling because of his acceleration, because you knew it was there any time you wanted it. He had a little thing he'd do, though, at the end of his gallops. When you would finish, walk forward and then turn around, no matter what you did he wheeled and spun around as fast as he could. That's how he dropped a lot of people. All of his riders in Europe. That's how he dropped me. Bill Shoemaker was on a horse right behind me at the time and got a good laugh.

"He had a massive front end, with a great angle to his shoulder," de Seroux went on, warming to the memory. "When you were sitting on his back, it seemed forever to get to his ears, because he had such a great length of neck. I think that's what gave him his balance and his length of stride, and compensated for his weaker hind end. His hocks were slightly 'away,' meaning they fell behind the ideal straight line from hip through hock. And you couldn't ignore the fact that he was knock-kneed. Charlie Whittingham said he walked like Charlie Chaplin.

"He wasn't afraid of anything," de Seroux added, "or intimidated by anything. Neither is Cigar. Palace Music had an imperious masculinity. They both have that one white eye. And Palace was very intelligent. When I walked into the barn he would scream his head off for me. There were times he would run you right out of his stall. But at Chantilly, where he was very relaxed, I used to go into his stall late in the morning and hug him. He would be as gentle as a lamb. We bonded there, and that's why it was so exciting for me to be on him later in California."

By the time Palace Music settled in for his first breeding season at Brookside, his aggressive personality had resurfaced.

"Palace Music was kind of a big, silly sonofabitch," Ted Carr said. "He could be kind of mean and nasty. Wanted to get to you. So Mac had to take him and round pen him. Put him to work, get him to hook onto you and be a partner rather than a bandido. The idea was to make him your friend instead of your enemy. After that he was fine. Never had any more trouble."

While Palace Music tried to be the center of attention, Solar Slew was quiet as a mouse. She ended up running seven times as a three-year-old in 1985 without winning a race. "She was never a very sound filly," McAnally said. "Fortunately, Allen was buying fillies with good family." By the end of 1985 Solar Slew's racing days were over. She was sent to Brookside to commence a life of motherhood as one of more than a hundred broodmares making up the Paulson nursery. Her second career had begun.

Even with her attractive breeding, Solar Slew had to take a backseat in the Brookside broodmare firmament when compared to such racing stars as Zalataia, L'Attrayante, Committed and Estrapade. They had proven themselves on the racetrack to such an extent that any sons or daughters they produced of note would be pure gravy. Solar Slew, on the other hand, had yet to justify her half-million dollar price tag. As an investment, she was close to becoming a write-off. Her first two foals were sold for small change to Latin American buyers who were impressed with the Argentine influence in her pedigree. One of them became a champion. Her third foal, a son of Paulson's Australian turf star Strawberry Road, was at her side in the spring of 1989 when it came time for another routine mating. This time, Ted Carr thought it would be a good idea to match Solar Slew with Palace Music, thereby mixing the blood of Seattle Slew and Northern Dancer. Their one and only intimate encounter took place on May 3 when the stocky, dark brown mare was led up to the Brookside Farm stallion complex. Soon afterwards Solar Slew was pronounced in foal.

Brookside is a pretty nice place to live if you're an expectant thoroughbred mare. Located near the town of Versailles, the property spreads across the gently rolling ground sitting on the west side of the most valuable stretch of State Highway 60 in Kentucky's Woodford County. With Ted Carr's advice and hands-on guidance, Brookside was built in 1985 after Paulson decided he wanted to create his own thoroughbred factory. At the time Paulson was spending his money to buy other people's horses. Eventually, he wanted to be self-sufficient. Paulson met Carr once, hired him on the spot, and turned him loose with the vague mandate: "I want a nice place for my horses. Build me a classic Kentucky farm." Carr was a second generation Kentucky horseman who had worked for a number of top breeding farms since the age of nineteen. He read between the lines and viewed the property as the canvas on which he could finally paint his own masterpiece. He recalled his first impressions:

"I'd spent a lifetime managing old farms that were built ass-backwards. So I really knew what not to do. How to lay one out so it would be more workable and more convenient.

I'd ride a horse around here, drive around and study the land, then come back and put it on paper. I like barns on higher spots so the water doesn't run in 'em. People don't pay attention to that, then they get in trouble. All our barns are well-drained, so we never have a water problem. This rolling land gave us that opportunity. And the hills, thank God, were kind of in the right place so you could lay a barn out with so many acres per barn, and so many paddocks per barn. Then run your roads through here—there were no roads on the property. And just make it real workable—and a pretty place, too. You've got to think of the aesthetics of it and try to make it nice. I didn't want to build it and make it look like a chicken coop."

By 1989 the farm had grown to more than fifteen hundred acres, laced with seventy-five miles of fence and nearly eight miles of internal roads. There were sixteen custom-built barns dotting the hilltops, each barn costing about $385,000. The barns featured polished wood paneling, brass railings and hardware, and sparkling crystal chandeliers hanging in the cupolas. Yes, chandeliers.

"Everyone thought it was extravagant," Paulson explained, almost apologetically. "Having chandeliers in the barns. What I wanted was a Spanish style, heavier looking kind of fixture. But they wanted way too much for those. Then I stumbled on this warehouse full of chandeliers at a great price. I thought, 'Why not?' I think they look great."

The original property included structures dating back to the late eighteenth century. A small stone building that once served as a slave quarters was converted into a guest cottage.

The main residence was originally built in 1790, then expanded in 1890. Carr added another wing in 1990 for the comfort of the Paulsons, who usually spend Kentucky Derby time at Brookside entertaining friends and family. Carr declined to speculate on who would handle the renovation in the year 2090, but he did add a tennis court near the residence. Soon after that, Paulson suggested a golf course.

"You say let there be a golf course, and there will be one," Carr told the boss. "But just so you know, the way I've got this place laid out I need every inch of land to go with these barns." Paulson bought the Del Mar Country Club in Southern California instead.

Solar Slew spent her gestation of 1989 at Brookside's equine country club, grazing in a three-acre meadow ripe with bluegrass and tasty clover. For most of the summer she had the company of her little one—he was later named Strawberry McSlew—along with the dozens of other Brookside mares growing heavy with foal. As the foal was weaned, however, and the new year approached, the decision was made to send Solar Slew and three of her companions to Maryland. The move was based purely on economics. Paulson had a twenty-five percent interest in two syndicated Maryland stallions—Allen's Prospect and Corridor Key. He wanted to support them with his mares, but not necessarily his best mares. Solar Slew fit the bill. And so, on February 13, 1990, Solar Slew and three companions—all great with foal—boarded a shiny aluminum Sallee horse van at Brookside and embarked upon the fourteen-hour ride to the venerable Country Life Farm, located deep in the Maryland countryside, about thirty miles northeast of Baltimore.

At Country Life the Paulson mares were given over to the care of the family Pons. Brothers Josh and Michael ran the place for their retired parents, Joe and Mary Jo. But retired was about the last word anyone would choose to describe this clan of passionate horse people. Twenty-four hours a day, three hundred and sixty-five days a year, Country Life teemed with all manner of equine life: mares in foal, mares giving birth, mares in waiting for stallions hot to breed. Young foals dotted the hilly landscape, from the entrance at Old Joppa Road to the vast, upper pasture overlooking Route 1 that drops off to dense woods and the chilled waters of a creek called Winters Run.

Josh Pons vaguely recalls the sight of the Sallee van pulling into Country Life with the Paulson mares that winter. Along with Solar Slew there was Harem Bound, a daughter of Pretense, and Kahaila, a daughter of Pitcairn—both in foal to Strawberry Road—and Positioned, a daughter of Cannonade who, like Solar Slew, was carrying a foal by Palace Music. But beyond the fact that Allen Paulson was a highly valued client, their arrival in Maryland was an unremarkable event. The farm was hopping with activity. That year alone more than forty foals came into this world at Country Life. At the same time, four young stallions needed daily attention to service their full dance cards. At night, Josh Pons would chain himself to his desk and record the essence of the day's events. He was in the midst of writing a journal for *The Blood-Horse* magazine that would later be published as *Country Life Diary: Three Years in the Life of a Horse Farm.*

Positioned was the first of the Paulson mares to foal. She gave birth to a filly on April 3. Two weeks later, on the evening of April 17, Solar Slew began showing signs that her time was near. She was led from the broodmare barn to the foaling barn, a small, two-stall wooden building with a steeply pitched roof covered in gray slate shingles. The barn was painted a glistening white, with window trim and doors a rich, brick red. Solar Slew entered the larger of the two stalls beneath the shelter of the little shedrow. The stall was twenty feet wide, fifteen feet deep, with a nine-foot ceiling and thick straw covering a well-worn wooden floor. A seventy-five watt bulb hanging overhead gave off a soft glow. Three heat lamps helped cut the evening chill. There was hay in a manger, a bucket of water, and a security camera mounted high in a corner.

For Richard Harris, it was a night just like any other night in foaling season. From his cottage just across the road from the foaling barn, the forty-five-year-old Harris was the man in charge when the mares entered labor. It was his responsibility to help with the birth and alert a vet if there were complications. By mid-April of 1990, Harris was only part way through one of the busiest foaling loads Country Life had ever seen. Sometimes there were two a night. Sometimes two more the next morning.

Harris was a native of Bluefield, West Virginia, who had been working at Country Life since the spring of 1983.

That's when Joe Pons, Josh's father, met Harris in a halfway house and gave him a job. Like Joe Pons, Harris was a recovering alcoholic. The elder Pons made it a point to help a fellow traveler whenever he could. In Harris, he bet on a man who had never before handled a horse.

Soon, though, it was apparent Harris had missed his calling. One by one, he mastered the various Country Life chores with the sure hand of a natural born horseman. Josh Pons described Harris as "our West Virginian who can outwork any four Marylanders." Eventually, there came the day a new man was needed in the foaling barn. Harris was the obvious choice. "It was a challenge," he recalled, speaking in a soft, flat West Virginia drawl that spared no extra syllables. "You're in there to help the mare pull the foal out if she needs it. Mostly, though, you're just quiet, keeping her calm." Sometimes Harris would sing. Nothing special. A lullaby, maybe, or a country song. It helped pass the time, and who's to say it didn't comfort the mare as she submitted to the pain and contractions of her labor. When the time came, Harris would pray for the sight of those front feet and that wet nose to appear first from the womb, signaling the glad sight of a normal birth.

Solar Slew went until nearly dawn on the morning of April 18 before her water broke. From that point on it was very routine. As Harris pulled in rhythm with the spasms of the mare and the foal's head followed, he noticed the curious, off-center blaze spreading halfway down the bridge of its nose. Seconds later Harris knew he had a colt. The time was 5:45 a.m. Cigar had entered the world.

Solar Slew and her new foal fell into a daily routine. Each morning they would be led from the barn to the upper pasture. Little Cigar would spend the day testing his long, unruly legs and sniffing out curious smells. He discovered the other new foals, playful creatures just like him. Then each evening they would be led home again, mother and son, side by side.

Ellen Pons, Josh's wife, was five months pregnant with their first child when Solar Slew's foal made his first permanent impression. It was Preakness week in Maryland, and Country Life was a Mecca for visitors in town to watch the second jewel in the Triple Crown. The Pons family welcomed the exciting interlude. Their party on the Thursday night before the race had become a great tradition. But the heavy social schedule took its toll on the everyday business of running the farm. No matter. Everyone pitched in. And Ellen, proud horsewoman and full time Pons, was not about to let her growing condition get in the way.

Late one afternoon, Ellen and two other farm hands headed out to the pasture to round up three sets of mares and their foals to bring them in for the night. For no particular reason, Ellen clipped her shank on Solar Slew's halter and gathered her white-faced colt alongside. As they walked down the gravel path that ran alongside the pond, Ellen and her companions were second in the procession. They had just reached a patch of wet grass when little Cigar squirmed away from Ellen and lashed out with a hind leg, catching her smack in the side of the stomach.

Ellen's first thought was, "Wow!" Her second was, "I'm okay." And then she turned her attention to the mischievous colt. "How did you do that?" she exclaimed. Little Cigar was trying hard to look innocent.

"I'd been working every day with him. I think he was just showing off." Ellen knew enough about horses to give a month-old foal the benefit of the doubt. "It was like, 'Watch this trick!' And then he held up at the last second. I said 'thank you' for the lesson and vowed never to take my eyes off him again." Ellen kept the incident to herself. It did not even make her husband's diaries. Four and a half months later, on October 1, Joseph Pons III was born with a dimple in his right cheek. Only his right cheek. His grandmother swears little Josh got it that day in May when Cigar said hello.

After delivering her healthy foal, Solar Slew's business at Country Life was not over. She was there to be bred at the first healthy opportunity to Corridor Key, who just happened to be a half-brother to Palace Music. She and Corridor Key needed three covers before the job was done, and then, on May 31, an ultrasound confirmed that she was in foal. Plans for the Paulson mares to return to Kentucky were postponed, however, when Solar Slew's foal came down with a respiratory infection. The colt recovered without fuss. He was wormed, his feet were trimmed, and he was given the normal schedule of inoculations. On Thursday, July 26, the four Paulson mares and their foals boarded a Sallee van for the journey back to Brookside Farm.

In subsequent years, as Cigar emerged from that nursery of

more than forty Country Life foals to become the most famous horse in the world, Josh Pons rifled through his diaries, searching for references. To his amazement, he found nothing specific, other than a description of the imposing vans pulling through the Country Life gates and off-loading their valuable cargo.

"I always remembered him as a good looking, good feeling colt that you kind of had to get a hold of when you led him out," Pons said. "But when it comes right down to it, I'm a populist. I like to treat all these horses the same. I've been teased about it, though. My editor said, 'Jeez, you had a Horse of the Year on the farm and you never even knew it?' The fact that there was no particular mention of Cigar as a foal is not really significant. We're certainly proud he was born here, of course. I like to think a farm is known by the company it keeps."

The *Country Life Diary* entry for July 27, 1990, records a phone call that day from Allen Paulson. The topic of conversation was his two-year-old colt Xray, who had won a race two days earlier at Del Mar. Xray was a son of the Country Life stallion Allen's Prospect. In the course of the conversation, Pons asked Paulson about the odd name:

"Oh, well, I have so many horses to name, I thought maybe I'd just name them for places important to me," Paulson replied. "I'm a pilot, you know. Flown around the globe several times. I named Xray for a checkpoint over Newfoundland, if I'm not mistaken. Most checkpoints are short names, and are so unique the Jockey Club has the name available."

Paulson had more than a hundred foals to name in 1990. Nearly all of them were named for one of those aviation checkpoints. The checkpoint Cigar is located about a hundred miles west of Tampa, Florida, in the Gulf of Mexico, at longitude twenty-seven degrees, twenty-eight minutes north, and latitude eighty-four degrees, forty-eight minutes west. But it was pure chance the Paulsons—both non-smokers—attached that name to that particular foal. The son of Solar Slew and Palace Music could have been called Skags, Kerki, or Skipo. Skipo! He could have been saddled with Cuffy, Tutts or Snupy. The other Country Life foals, all fillies, were eventually named Reni, Vidaca and Auila, appropriately feminine and slightly exotic. But Cigar, one of the boys, could just as easily have been named Wamps, Blako or Uckie. Consider for a moment this headline from hell: "Uckie Wins Breeders' Cup Classic!"

There were many checkpoint names attached to the Paulson foals of 1990 that played more pleasantly in the ear. Cigar could have been Cosby (talk about a television hook) or Magma (boiling, unstoppable), or even named Cugar or Cheta, summoning images of ferocity and speed. Of course, the best horses tend to overcome even the most awkward names. And in that crop of 1990, Paulson had the best bunch of young thoroughbreds he ever bred...no matter what they were called.

Take Cigar out of that foal crop and still there was a core group of millionaires, major winners, and even two starters in the 1993 Kentucky Derby, Diazo and Corby. Diazo ran a respectable fifth and Corby, already a major stakes winner, finished right behind his classmate in sixth. The following year, Diazo won the $500,000 Strub Stakes, while Stuka was awarded victory in the $1-million Santa Anita Handicap on the disqualification of the original winner. Madeleine's Dream, a daughter of champion Theatrical, went abroad and won the classic French One Thousand Guineas. Vinista stayed home and became a stakes winner on the grass. But the queen of them all was Eliza, a daughter of Mt. Livermore. Eliza burst onto the scene during the summer of 1992, quick as a Spitfire and graceful as a ballet dancer. She won major stakes races in Chicago and Kentucky, and then ended her season with a victory in the $1-million Breeders' Cup Juvenile Fillies at Gulfstream Park. Eliza became the Paulsons' first champion bred by Brookside Farm.

When Solar Slew and her son arrived at Brookside, they slipped smoothly into the well-oiled routine that Ted Carr prescribed for all mares and foals. After spending their nights in the pasture they were brought to the barn at seven o'clock in the morning, then turned out again about three hours later. While in the barn, the foals were tied to their stall wall and gently handled to allay their fears. They were brushed and fussed over like little kings and queens. Their feet were inspected, picked and cleaned. After awhile, they grew accustomed to all of the attention. Those who did not would have trouble later on. It was their first lesson toward the higher education of becoming a racehorse.

Solar Slew, her foal, and the others who had come in from Maryland spent the summer to themselves in their own private field. With the health of a hundred foals at stake, there was no such thing as being too cautious in the prevention of possible infection from outside sources. In the meantime, Solar Slew's foal had picked up a nickname, as well as a bit of a schizophrenic reputation. The farm hands called him The Hammer, inspired by his inclination to strike out with his front feet. Ellen Pons could have attested to the perils of the hind end, and later, in California, exercise riders would hang on for dear life as the two-year-old version of Cigar would rear up and paw the air. But there were also those at Brookside who never had a moment's trouble with the little son of Palace Music. As far as they were concerned, he just as easily could have been called The Pro.

By early October it was time to wean the foals from their mothers. Gradually, the mares were withdrawn from the pasture until the foals looked around one day to discover that they were on their own. The Hammer and his Maryland pals had a field to themselves at the north end of the Brookside spread, on property recently acquired from neighboring Pin Oak Farm. It was a good life, and the little ones were cutting loose, testing their competitive instincts and stretching their increasingly stronger legs. Occasionally, they would get into trouble.

On the night of October 10, or early the next morning, a deer must have bounded over the pasture fence and spooked the foals something awful. At least, that is what Ted and Mac Carr figure happened. The foals ran amok, colliding with railings, posts and trees in the dark. The next morning Brookside foreman Mike Barber discovered the carnage. Some of the foals were scraped and bleeding, but they would live to fight another day. Little Cigar, on the other hand, stood quivering as Barber approached. Something was terribly wrong. A broad flap of skin dangled from the colt's right shoulder. The gaping wound was already clotted with blood. Barber immediately radioed for help.

Over the next several weeks, Mac Carr got to know little Cigar intimately. The gash had been stitched together at a local clinic, but the tissue was too weak to hold the stitches in place. Mac took a pair of scissors and cut them out, then commenced a routine of pressure hosing and applications of Scarlet Oil, an astringent that helped close the wound and enhance healing. The colt was intelligent enough to submit without protest. Soon, The Hammer went back into the general population. Only now he was marked with a nasty scar to go along with his distinctive blaze.

In 1990, Mac Carr took over the breaking of the Brookside yearlings from his father. It was a dream job, rife with pressure and responsibility. The lessons learned by the young horses would be imprinted forever. Bad habits would haunt them and good behavior would help make them better racehorses. "Mac is like my second skin," Ted said when he passed the baton to his son. "I couldn't have a better man at the job."

The Carrs practiced a philosophy of cowboy horseman-ship that links man and beast in a cooperative venture. Instead of punishment there is encouragement. Instead of brute handling there is subtle guidance. Ted Carr was a life-long disciple of the legendary Ray Hunt, whose techniques of handling young horses became a model for the most successful modern trainers of performance animals. "Years ago you'd think of maybe using a two-by-four to get their attention," Ted Carr said, harking back to the bad old days. "But the older you get, you learn it works best the softer and gentler you do it." Both Carrs kept a photo of Ray Hunt in their Brookside offices.

Cigar—he was still known as "the Solar Slew"—was assigned to set number three of the four Brookside training groups that entered the yearling breaking process in the fall of 1991. There were thirty yearlings in Cigar's set, including the young horses who would later become Eliza and Corby, as well as his old pal Reni from Country Life Farm. They had never felt a saddle. They had never tasted a bit. School began for the leery, wide-eyed bunch in set number three on Saturday, October 5, and continued for the next forty-five days. And they all started with the same set of expectations, family considerations aside.

"Of course, you didn't think of the Palace Musics then of being our future Triple Crown horses or champions, if we were to have any," Ted Carr said. "But when we break them, they're all just alike. No matter how they're bred, who they're by or out of, we're gonna treat 'em all the same. We want them broke just like a gentle riding pony."

Cigar learned his lessons well. Mac Carr's detailed notebook of the breaking of set number three singles out the problem students, the slow-learners and the budding juvenile delinquents. The yearlings went through a progression of wall work, figure eights, stall riding, pen work, and eventually jogs and gallops. Eliza needed time away from the group to ride quietly over the hills. After that, she was okay. One of the fillies "froze up" just three days into the training. Another got tagged with a "bad attitude" after a week of work and spent most of the month in the doghouse. This colt was "flighty" and that one was just plain "silly"—all of them listed by the name of their dams. At no point was the Solar Slew mentioned at all.

"The only ones that stand out in your mind are the ones who are a pain in the butt," Mac Carr said. "Cigar was kind of my type, a big ol' pretty bay thing. And really laid back. Give you an example. My riders don't think much like me. They're always rough on horses. They don't listen and they don't want to learn. They'd tell me you couldn't do this or couldn't do that with one of these yearlings because they're racehorses, not work horses. I got tired of listening to it, so one day I jumped on Cigar bareback. 'See, you can do anything you want,' I said, then rode him around like he'd been doing it all his life. He was a real smart horse."

Graduation day was Friday, November 15. All thirty yearlings from Brookside set number three were loaded onto vans, driven to Lexington's Bluegrass Airport, and flown twenty-three hundred miles across country to Ontario International Airport in suburban Los Angeles. Cigar was on the move again. Next stop—the racetrack.

CHAPTER 2

AIRBORNE

Allen Paulson was having a chat with some newfound racing friends in a cocktail lounge when a man approached and slapped his fine leather briefcase on the bar.

"Mr. Paulson, in here I have a classic filly," said the man, patting the briefcase with loving affection. "A Grade I racehorse and a broodmare prospect. A filly you will want to own."

Paulson was feeling puckish. It was a tune he had heard before. He glanced down at the case, then back at the man. A smile toyed with the corners of his mouth. His pale blue eyes gleamed with mischief in mind.

"Well," Paulson replied, his soft voice halting for effect, "maybe you'd better let her out."

The salesman was hardly discouraged. Inevitably, he would come back for more. The year was 1983, at the height of the worldwide thoroughbred bloodstock boom, and Paulson was a marked man. He might as well have been wearing a bull's-eye painted on the back of his golf slacks. Every thoroughbred breeder with a decent horse knew his name. Every bloodstock agent in the game had his number. Whenever Paulson walked into a sales pavilion, a shedrow or a racetrack clubhouse, he trailed a scent of available money. He was a man building a thoroughbred dream, and he was building it fast.

He was also hard to figure, far from the eighties image of

the swashbuckling corporate superstar in full, Reagan-era ascendancy. When Paulson's resume preceded him into a room, people would gasp at a ledger displaying the tale of a $52-million investment for a struggling corporate jet company that in just five years was turned into half a billion dollar stock offering and $89 million in cash. They would brace themselves to behold the daredevil test pilot who flew his own sleek aircraft at record-setting speeds. They were ready for an overwhelming presence that combined John Wayne and John Galt, with starlets on his arm, a full grill of blinding, white teeth emerging from a deep tan, and a wardrobe cut to fit a physique designed by Michelangelo.

Well, at least they were right about the starlets. Linda Evans, with "The Big Valley" behind her and "Dynasty" on the rise, was a frequent Paulson companion. There was also Donna Douglas, better known in her high-profile days as Ellie Mae Clampett of TV's "Beverly Hillbillies." Others appeared at his side, immediately drawing attention away from the man himself. The reaction was unfailingly amusing: "Oooh, ahhh, look there!" and then, "Huh? That's Allen Paulson?"

He could have been lost in a crowd of Iowa farmers—which his father was—or among a bunch of grease-monkeys leaning into an engine, their hands grimy and fingers thick from constant abuse from gears and close tolerances. Paulson presented the world with an open, placid countenance, devoid of guile or conflicted thought. By the early 1980s his fair hair was in full retreat, and his broad, working man's frame was carrying a bit more weight than he wanted. In motion he remained nimble, light and forward on his feet. His voice was soft and hesitant, playing like an untrained version of fellow Corn Belt native Ronald Reagan—only with the volume turned way down low.

Paulson did not hesitate to play his mild-mannered image for all it was worth, yet he built his empire by being deeply competitive, possessed of a thoroughly macho pride in thumping the other guy. As a salesman, he was quietly insistent, backing his pitch with the proven quality of his Gulfstream products. A customer could ask, "How do you know?" Paulson could reply, "Because I build them and fly them myself." And up they would go. As a manager, he preached a gospel of Norman Vincent Peale blended with Teddy Roosevelt: "Think positively, walk softly, and carry a big stick."

Paulson's big stick was an unshakable confidence in his own instincts, and his enduring faith in the efficacy of hard, steady work. He began building and expanding aircraft companies in 1951, putting in long days to make them fly. His mantra was, from an early age, "I've never met a lazy lucky guy." And he proved it time and time again until, by 1984, his net worth approached half a billion dollars.

By the early 1980s, Paulson could look back upon more than thirty years of relentless success in one of the world's most competitive industries. Why should the thoroughbred business be any different? Paulson toyed with the game in the late 1960s as part of a claiming partnership. But that was no fun. The risk, though relatively slight, did not create any tangible rewards. Neither did he have the time to immerse himself in the workings of the game. He got out quickly and vowed not to return until he could afford to play at the top. That moment occurred in April of 1983, when he took Gulfstream Aerospace Technologies public. The Gulfstream offering was 8.8 million shares, largest by an American company since Ford sold more than ten million in 1955. Paulson sold 4.7 million shares from his own holdings at $19 a share for a cool $89.3 million in cash. He retained about seventy percent of the company, some 24.3 million shares, worth another $461.7 million at the time. Wall Street placed the total book value of Gulfstream Aerospace at $630 million.

Suddenly, Paulson had both the will and the way to try the horses again. He began with a plan that was geared for the long haul. Accustomed to building on a grand scale, he envisioned a sweeping vista of beautiful animals set against a storybook Kentucky background. He foresaw the day when his business life was less hectic, when tennis and golf no longer held their recreational allure, when the thoroughbreds would be the most important diversion in his life. But he had no family traditions, no bluegrass blood running through his veins. Anything he created would be spun from his own whole cloth. He wanted to win the most famous races, starting with the Kentucky Derby and its Triple Crown sisters, the Preakness and Belmont Stakes. He wanted someday to say he was breeding his own champions, just as he crafted his remarkable Gulfstream jets. He wanted to build a thoroughbred organization that hummed with efficiency and took pride in its product. He wasn't exactly sure how to do it, but he knew he wanted the best.

So Paulson started buying thoroughbreds, and buying them with an abandon that rivaled the spending sprees of the Middle Eastern sheikhs. His philosophy was simple, honed on lessons learned in aerospace. Spending top dollar on the best products will—when properly managed—net the greatest rewards. In short, he was seeking the equine equivalents of the Gulfstream jets, with their gold-plated fixtures, silk carpets, sophisticated hardware and $25-million price tags. In 1983, when the ink was barely dry on the Gulfstream deal, Paulson spent $11.8 million on yearlings and two-year-olds at public auctions alone. In 1984 he paid another $11 million for the same kind of high-end product. In 1985 Paulson pulled back on the throttle and spent nearly $20 million, with more than $17 million of the total exclusively on risky yearlings.

The early 1980s represented the boom in the Northern Dancer craze, when mind-boggling sums were being paid for the sons and daughters of the incomparable stallion. Paulson did his homework and knew in general which horses looked best on paper. He admitted no knowledge of conformation and relied upon a cadre of advisors. He figured, though, that the animals being auctioned at the most exclusive sales were already the cream of the crop. In July of 1984 he went to $8 million in the bidding on a son of Northern Dancer, then was topped by a bid of $8.25 million. "Eight million was high enough," Paulson said at the time. "I really was only going to five million, but I kind of got carried away." There were plenty of others to satisfy Paulson's hunger. If he was outbid for a son or a daughter of Northern Dancer, he settled for the next best thing: a son or daughter of a son of Northern Dancer. Between 1983 and 1987, Paulson purchased two hundred and ten thoroughbreds at public auction and scores more in private transactions and package partnerships.

Soon Paulson had one of the most enviable racing inventories in the world, with a pattern skewed toward well-bred females whose value lasted long after they retired from the track. Paulson had the blood, the bones and the DNA to create his own thoroughbred empire. In competition, however, his horses were lagging far behind their investment. These four-legged Gulfstreams were barely getting off the ground. Paulson gambled on, but the intangibles of training, racing, injury and inherent soundness were becoming difficult lessons. In the beginning, Paulson was known more for his red ink than his blue ribbons and gold cups.

There was Mistral Dancer, a son of Northern Dancer, bought for $2.7 million. His earnings on the track: zero. He was sold to New Zealand at a huge loss. There was Nijinsky's Best, a daughter of Northern Dancer's best son Nijinsky. She cost Paulson $2.1 million and never made it to the races. There was Allen's Alydar, purchased as a weanling for $950,000. He went to England to be a racehorse and lapsed into anonymity. There was Anandar, another son of Alydar, who cost $750,000 as a two-year-old, started only four times, and never won a race. There was Daphne's Dancer, a daughter of Northern Dancer, whose racetrack earnings of $18,820 did not make much of a dent on her $1.05 million purchase price. And there was Solar Slew, whose competitive earnings of $5,856 did not even pay for her feed, let alone her $510,000 price tag.

Such early disappointments required a thick skin and strict commitment to a long-range goal. It did not take Paulson long to learn that the bloodstock trade was like swimming in a great ocean, with all its ebbs and flows. High tide on one beach means dry sand somewhere else. Paulson consoled himself with the public exploits of such readymade runners as Massera, L'Attrayante and Icehot. He got his greatest thrills when the big numbers hit: Savannah Dancer, a $2.5-million filly, won the Del Mar Oaks. Savannah Slew, who cost $470,000, won five stakes and set a track record. Northern Aspen became a bargain at $410,000 when she won a major grass race to enhance her long-term value as a broodmare.

In addition, there were some surprising nuggets to emerge from the huge inventory. The best of them was Daring Bidder, an unassuming yearling who cost Paulson just $125,000, mothered three stakes winners—including champion Eliza—and produced another foal that sold for $1.25 million.

"I've never known a business that relies so much on luck as horse racing," Paulson would tell close friends. "In other businesses you can reduce the risk and anticipate things with a lot more precision. With horse racing, you never know quite what can happen next."

Paulson had a penchant for the unpredictable himself. He never left the headlines for long. Both the racing industry and the larger business world seemed eternally fascinated by his contrasting images. On the one hand there were Paulson's flamboyant deals and high-flying Gulfstreams. On the other was his quiet, shy public persona. In 1985 he sold his share in the company to Chrysler Corporation for $636 million. A few months later he spent a record $4.5 million to buy out his partners in the classy mare Estrapade. In June of 1987 he captained a crew that flew a Gulfstream IV westbound around the world in record time. Nine months later he did the same thing in the other direction. And yet, at the same time, Paulson would query an acquaintance about the aesthetic impact of his racing silks—red, white and blue, emblazoned with patriotic stars and stripes, with a racy "GA" on the front, for Gulfstream Aerospace. "Do you think they might be too loud?" he asked, worried that he was showing off.

It was a typical Paulson statement, symptomatic of a life spent calling attention to his deeds and not to himself. He was low key by nature but extremely careful on purpose, a lesson he learned during the heyday of Gulfstream's growth in sleepy Savannah, Georgia, when Paulson's company was the biggest employer in town. News stories of record profits and multi-million dollar stock deals lured dark forces out of the woodwork. An attempt to kidnap Paulson's youngest son Michael was foiled by Michael himself, who used a derringer to kill one of his assailants. Paulson still has the ransom tape, delivered in advance.

For a time after that, Paulson carried a gun and watched his back. On a trip to Los Angeles, where Michael had moved after the kidnap attempt, Paulson and his driver had a scare one night when they were certain they were being pursued. Some evasive driving shook the suspicious tail, but Paulson refused to let down his guard. Still, there were times tragedy seemed to single him out. Why else would one of the world's great aerospace pioneers suffer the death of a son in a small plane crash in Montana?

Paulson had been married and divorced twice when he said yes to a blind date with the sister of the wife of a friend in the fall of 1983. He was late for dinner. She was not impressed.

"That first date was a catastrophe," Madeleine Paulson said. The memory lingered. "There was nothing. No connection. We arranged a game of tennis about a month later, but it rained, so we couldn't play. We stayed inside all afternoon, shooting pool and talking. It turned out to be the most wonderful day of my life. I fell in love, and I knew then that I would marry him."

When she met the man behind Gulfstream Aerospace, Madeleine Farris—her family name—was a former Pan American airline stewardess who ran her own business providing cabin service crews for corporate jets and special charter flights. Much of her business was done with people who owned Gulfstreams. Like Paulson, she was recently divorced, and the mother of a three-year-old daughter, named Dominique.

"When we met he had just bought the first of his yearlings,"

Madeleine recalled. "I knew nothing about horses, apart from the fact that they were beautiful. That first day together he showed me a picture of Savannah Dancer. He was so proud. He told me he was getting into horse racing because, as he matured and changed his lifestyle, he wanted to have something he could enjoy that would also be interesting and challenging."

Allen and Madeleine set off together on an adventure that revolved around racehorses, racetracks and the creation of homes and farms in California and Kentucky. Allen was an inveterate shutterbug, snapping photos wherever they traveled, harvesting ideas for gardens and architectural details. They discovered in each other an inclination to shy away from the party circuit, preferring to stay at home, eat in, and perhaps entertain a few close friends. Allen loved his poker and his gin rummy. Madeleine maintained her low handicap in golf and drew him deeper into the game. They both loved dogs. Lots of dogs. Upon the occasion of their wedding in 1988, Madeleine presented Allen with a white standard poodle puppy. He immediately went out and bought its brother. Madeleine's permanent sidekick was a possessive Jack Russell terrier named Oliver.

When they appeared at the races together, the Paulsons gave off an air of wealth and upper class *noblesse oblige*. Allen, in his sober business suits, deferred to Madeleine's designer fashions, which included an array of spectacular hats. There was the furry Russian look at the freezing '88 Breeders' Cup in Kentucky. There was the vast awning in tropical pink for a balmy Breeders' Cup in Florida. At the '95 Breeders' Cup, in honor of Cigar, Madeleine donned a splendid black edifice that discouraged approach. And in working-class Boston, for Cigar's 1996 Massachusetts Handicap, she pleased the fans with a creamy confection of silk and delicate lace.

"Hey, Madeleine. Nice lampshade!" came the cries from the raucous crowd. Madeleine was happy to oblige.

"They should see me the rest of the week," she said. "We lead a very normal life. I always get dressed for the races, though. I think it's an important part of the tradition. They are very special, those animals. If you can't dress for them there's nothing else to dress for. Especially Cigar. I always loved the way people would get dressed up to see Cigar."

As Cigar began to blossom as a star, the story of Allen Paulson's ancient history became intriguing to a new generation of journalists. He would deflect most probes, offering short answers like, "I didn't have much money. I was mostly on my own. I had to work pretty hard." He preferred to talk about his horses, especially Cigar. Of course, compared to Paulson, Cigar was raised like Little Lord Fauntleroy.

Allen Eugene Paulson was born on April 22, 1922, on his family's forty-acre farm just outside the town of Clinton, Iowa. Clinton was a Mississippi River port, population twenty-five thousand, full of granaries, feed lots and rail yards busy with the commerce of corn, wheat and beef cattle. Beyond that, it was known as the birthplace of stage star Lillian Russell, but little else.

Clinton was hit with the first ripples of the Great Depression before the rest of America went to its knees after the stock market crash of 1929. As corn prices plummeted, the Paulson family struggled. Allen remembers his mother, Lillian, burning surplus corn seed for fuel because it cost so much less than coal, and they had plenty of it lying around. By 1934, his father, Harry Paulson, gave up the struggle and hit the road. His oldest boys were grown and able to fend for themselves. Lillian Paulson was tubercular and on her way to a sanitarium. Young Allen, suddenly abandoned, faced a new life that held more nightmare than hope. He had to grow up fast.

On his own at age thirteen, Paulson found work in the Home Hotel in downtown Clinton. He scrubbed the floors, cleaned the toilets, and lived in a spartan room. He delivered newspapers, washed cars, and sold scrap metal on the side. When he was not in school he was always at some kind of work, except for those rare times he went for a swim at the YMCA or took in a picture at the local movie house. Had he come of age in Clinton, Paulson could have gone to work for the Clinton Corn Company, or the Bennett Box Company, or even the brand new DuPont cellophane plant just down the road in the town of Camanche. But Paulson, even as a high school freshman, was determined to find a way out of town. He dreamed of California.

"I was ready to go, but I couldn't afford the bus fare," Paulson recalled. "My dad was working at a ranch out there, somewhere north of San Francisco. He wrote and said if I could find a way out there he could help me find a job. I wasn't too close to my dad, but it sounded pretty good to me. Then one day at the movies I won the bingo prize. The jackpot was a hundred dollars, but there were two other winners, so we had to split it three ways. I took my $33.30 to the Greyhound Bus Station the next day and bought a ticket to San Francisco."

Paulson's father made good on his promise. Before too long, Allen was working on a ranch near the town of Marshall, California, located about sixty miles north of San Francisco, just inland from the rocky Pacific Coast. Paulson, fifteen and feeling free, took a deep breath of clean, country air and dove into his new life with enthusiasm.

Although he discovered he had a way with the horses, cattle and various types of farm machinery, Paulson's youthful passion was saved for airplanes. On weekend breaks from work at the ranch he would hitch joy rides with local stunt pilots between their barnstorming air shows. Late at night he would build model planes of his own design, using bamboo, balsa wood and scraps of cloth. Paulson even participated in the rescue effort of the mysterious crash of United Airlines Trip 6, a DC-3 carrying eight passengers and crew that strayed wildly off course, ran out of fuel, and plunged into the rough waters off Northern California on the night of November 28, 1938. The ranch was only twenty miles away. Paulson heard the news of the crash early the next morning and rushed to the site. Nearly sixty years later, the memory was still vivid.

"When I got there the Coast Guard was trying to get to the plane before it broke up on the rocks," Paulson said. "I stripped and swam out there. The wings had already broken off by the time I got there, but the cabin was dry inside. We learned later that the captain had told everybody to get up on the fuselage after they ditched. All but two of them were washed off and drowned. If they had stayed inside they would have survived."

Inside the plane, Paulson found a bag of mail and the captain's hat. He dove back in the icy waters and headed for shore. Waiting there was a newspaper photographer who had climbed down the steep cliff with the rescuers to get a better view of the action. Paulson, cold and tired, smiled for the camera.

"In the paper the next day, they ran the picture," Paulson recalled. "Underneath it said, 'Captain Saves the Mail.' What they didn't know is that my clothes had been carried out by the tide. When I got to the top of the cliff, after leading a bunch of people up from the beach, there was a whole crowd waiting for us. And there I was in my skivvies!"

Back at the ranch, the cattle had him up at dawn and back home after sunset. The cow ponies were hard-working and fun to ride. In between he attended Tomales High School, where he played on the football team and did well in mathematics. Literature, history and composition did not come quite so easily, but Paulson graduated, and soon he was heading south to Oakland to work for Trans World Airlines as an entry-level mechanic at thirty cents an hour. One of his jobs was to make sure there was a plane ready at a moment's notice for TWA's eccentric head man, Howard Hughes.

Paulson took advantage of a special training plan and spent a year studying engineering at the University of West Virginia. World War II pulled him into the Army Air Corps, where he received intensive flight deck training on domestic runs. After the war it was back to TWA and the booming world of aerospace. Paulson earned a reputation as a clear thinker with top-notch mechanical skills and an ability to see through knotty problems. Before long, he was promoted to flight crew engineer and spent most of his time in the air.

Back on the ground, Paulson made the most of his down time. He had his own workshop in Burbank, California, near his home. After an eight-hour day at TWA he would spend another six hours in his own shop. To his wife and three young sons he was a big, pleasant figure who made an occasional appearance between workshop sessions and cross-country flights. Paulson borrowed $1,500 from the TWA credit union, bought a surplus B-29 engine, and stripped it down to learn the innermost workings of its parts. He came up with the idea to plate the inside of piston cylinders with hard chrome to prevent intrusion by foreign particles. He modified a pressure valve that had been giving engineers fits. And he figured out how to fix a lubrication problem that had been plaguing the usually reliable Wright 3350 engines common to most carriers. Paulson took his idea to TWA, but TWA balked. Undaunted, Paulson sold the modifications to other airlines. Eventually, TWA went along and paid for the technology they could have had for free.

By then, Paulson's sideline business had grown strong enough for him to form his first company specializing in spare parts and refitting. He called it California Airmotive Corporation. In 1953 he resigned from TWA to devote all his energies to his own ventures. He would never work for anyone else again. Ensuing signposts in the Paulson odyssey plot a road map to nearly seamless success. In the late 1950s the exciting new Learjet caught his eye. Arnold Palmer was flying one. So were a growing class of corporate titans, opening up a grand vista of marketing opportunities. Paulson contracted to become Learjet's main distributor, but he knew the key was in creating the product. Bitten by the bug of the private jet world, he formed American Jet Industries in 1970 and developed the Hustler, designed with a prop in front for short runways and a jet in back for high-altitude cruising.

The Hustler led Paulson to make an offer to buy the General Aviation division of Rockwell International, located in Oklahoma City. At the same time, he learned that Grumman Aerospace Corporation was looking to sell its Gulfstream corporate jet division, complete with its factory in Savannah. Paulson could hardly control his excitement.

"I got in my Learjet and flew down there immediately," Paulson said. "I never dreamed Gulfstream would be put up for sale. I was like a kid in a candy store. I was afraid I was going to blow it because I was so eager to buy it." With the help of E. F. Hutton, Paulson came up with $52 million to buy both Rockwell's General Aviation and Grumman's Gulfstream companies. Together they became Gulfstream Aerospace, makers of the most coveted private jet in the world.

The new company could say, without fear of contradiction, that a ride in a Gulfstream was like an evening in a cozy, elegant salon. Flying at forty-four thousand feet, high above commercial traffic, and purring along at nearly five hundred miles per hour, the experience attacked modern business-men and government leaders at their most vulnerable pressure points: time and comfort. Time was reduced through the Gulfstream's speed and efficiency. Comfort was enhanced by customized cabins that catered to every conceivable personal whim. When Paulson introduced new Gulfstream buyers to their sparkling machines, he would beam like a proud father at a child's graduation. At around $25 million a jet, there was a lot of pride to go around.

After the acquisition, Paulson pressed on with the development of the Gulfstream III generation, and for the next four years he worked like a maniac. In 1982, E. F. Hutton grew itchy and demanded Paulson go public to enhance their investment. Paulson balked, knowing in his gut that the following year would be Gulfstream's best year yet and therefore a much better time for an offering. He rebuffed Hutton and bought out their ten percent stake at $8.50 a share. One year later, Gulfstream went public at $19 per share.

"For some reason I've always seemed to have pretty good instincts about when to make a move and when to wait," Paulson explained. "The real trick, too, is knowing when to get out. I had to do that with Wheeling steel. I had to do that with the car dealerships in L.A. And I've had to do that with horses and farms. If you keep things too long, they can drag down the rest."

While he was busy with one hand bidding on expensive thoroughbreds, Paulson bought a one-third interest in Wheeling-Pittsburgh Steel Corporation in 1983, spending about $50 million of his hard-earned Gulfstream profits. Two years later, when it became painfully apparent the American steel industry would not rebound, the company filed for Chapter 11 bankruptcy protection. The following year Paulson dumped his stake for $13.5 million.

"For better or worse, money is how success is measured in this society," Paulson said. "I've never really looked at money as what it could buy for me. It's more like a way of keeping score. And I learned how to keep score pretty young, playing pinochle with those old guys at the hotel where I worked."

It is a good thing Paulson didn't need a quick hundred thousand bucks in the spring of 1993. That is when Eddie Gregson, the man who trained 1982 Kentucky Derby winner Gato Del Sol, showed interest in a fifty percent partnership in Cigar at that price. Paulson's agent came back at $150,000, and Gregson turned down the deal.

"He had just broken his maiden," Gregson recalled without regrets. "At a hundred thousand, I was interested. At one-fifty, he was overvalued, I thought, for a Palace Music who really hadn't done anything yet. You can't be second-guessing yourself in this business or you'll go crazy."

By the time Cigar reached the races, Paulson's thoroughbred empire had spread, quite literally, from coast to coast. No other American-owned stable of thoroughbreds involved so many people in so many different places. In California, there was Brookside Farm West, where older horses were rested and young horses trained. In Kentucky there was Brookside Farm North, the nursery, home to the Paulson mares and stallions. In Ocala, Florida, there was the recently purchased Brookside Farm South, which would eventually be phased in to take the place of the West Coast training operation. Most of Paulson's horses raced with the Bill Mott stables in either New York or Kentucky, while a handful still raced in California.

There had been a few strategic setbacks along the way. Paulson's first attempt to build a California farm, near the inland city of Winchester, was thwarted by an easement issue that was not worth the fight. In 1992, on the strength of his success in big races for the Paulsons, Patrick Valenzuela was hired to ride first call for the stable. Less than a year later, Valenzuela's earlier history of drug dependency reared its head and the contract was terminated. And then there was Paulson's never-ending struggle to secure a full-time racing manager for his California horses.

His initial recruit was Dr. Jack Robbins, the internationally respected veterinarian whose first California clients had included the Calumet Farm horses of Ben Jones in the late 1940s. Among the horses on his daily rounds was Citation, who came to California that winter of 1949 on a fifteen-race winning streak. Paulson asked how much Robbins would charge to manage the stable, advise on buying and selling, communicate with trainers, and in general help protect him from lurking charlatans. Robbins considered the scope of the challenge and named his price.

"What?" Paulson gasped. The figure was $180,000. "That's more than I pay my president at Gulfstream!"

Robbins ended up advising on some of Paulson's earliest purchases—including Daring Bidder—while Ron McAnally, on his way to the Hall of Fame, trained most of Paulson's first runners. When Brookside Farm West was built, Paulson hired trainer George Scott full time. Scott quit for health reasons, and the job went to John Gosden, who already had a busy public stable. Within the year, Gosden began making plans to return to his native England to train for Sheikh Mohammed Al Maktoum.

At the end of 1988, as Gosden packed to leave, Paulson hired Richard Lundy, whose portfolio included several years at the right hand of Charlie Whittingham and a successful stint as a private trainer for Virginia Kraft Payson. Lundy set up shop at Brookside Farm, and in his first full year with Paulson the stable produced Blushing John, the champion older horse of 1989. The Lundy era came to an abrupt end in July of 1992 when Paulson discovered what he believed to be a kick-back scheme on the sale of horses involving Lundy and an outside agent. Paulson demanded Lundy's resignation, and although criminal charges never were brought, Paulson eventually won a long, drawn-out civil court battle that found in his favor.

At that point, Cigar was a two-year-old training at Brookside West, more than two years away from even scratching the surface of his destiny. That did not matter at all. As far as Paulson was concerned, he already owned the best horse in the world. That horse's name was Arazi.

The little red colt with the off-center stripe down his face was purchased at a Keeneland auction by Paulson as a weanling, late in 1989, for $350,000. He was named for an aviation checkpoint in Arizona and sent to France to be trained by Francois Boutin, one of Europe's classic horsemen. After losing his debut on May 30, 1991, Arazi won six consecutive races, including the four most important French events for two-year-olds, culminating with the Grand Criterium on the first Saturday in October at historic Longchamp.

One month later, Boutin brought Arazi to Kentucky to run in the Breeders' Cup Juvenile at Churchill Downs. No foreign-trained two-year-old had ever won a Breeders' Cup prize. The little colt responded with a breathtaking sweep through the large field that took everyone—even the Paulsons—by surprise. Suddenly alone in front with nearly a quarter of a mile to run, Arazi turned the race into a celebration. Fans hung out of the huge grandstands, screaming and applauding as Arazi danced past. He was, perhaps, the best two-year-old anyone had seen since the days of the great filly Ruffian. Arazi had barely caught his breath before he was anointed as the favorite for the Kentucky Derby the following May.

Alas, Arazi's knees required surgery after the Breeders' Cup, and his comeback in the spring of 1992 was rushed. Arazi arrived in Louisville to a media reception that rivaled the Super Bowl or the World Series. He trained in a fishbowl and had to be quarantined to ensure any moments of peace. In the race itself, Arazi ran as hard as he could for as far as he could and then, tired and spent, he finished eighth in the field of eighteen. The bubble had burst.

In the wake of the Derby disaster, Paulson took a lot of the blame. "I thought he could do it. I know it was asking a lot of him, but I thought he was just such a great horse that he could overcome everything. If I had it to do over again, I probably should have left him in Kentucky after his knee operation and let him train here for the Derby. But I felt a lot of loyalty to Francois. And I still think Arazi is a great horse. I hope he gets a chance to prove it."

Arazi managed to win again in France during the autumn of 1992, but he never recaptured the brilliance of his two-year-old season. That fall he returned to America to run in the Breeders' Cup Mile at Gulfstream Park and failed again. Soon after, Arazi was retired.

Paulson was deflated. Arazi, he felt, was a once in a lifetime thoroughbred. At the age of seventy, Paulson doubted that he would ever rise to such heights again.

"I always felt there was a big letdown after we had Arazi," Madeleine Paulson said. "I think that's when Allen tended not to take as much interest in the game. He'd say, 'After you've had an Arazi, what else is there?'"

CHAPTER 3

FRUSTRATION

Alex Hassinger does not remember the first time he noticed Cigar. There were simply too many gorgeous Paulson horses flooding into the Brookside West training center in Bonsall, California, that winter of 1991 for any one of them to stand out from the crowd. Hassinger will insist, however, with his hand on the Bible and an oath on his lips, that once he focused firmly on the dark bay colt with the distinctive swagger he would never, ever confuse him with another horse. Even as a callow two-year-old, Cigar had too much personality and too much presence to ignore. Of course, there was also Hassinger's indelible memory of Palace Music. You never quite forget a horse once he has tried to kill you.

"It was in Chicago, in 1986, while I was working for Charlie Whittingham," Hassinger began, still amazed he got out alive. "I was rubbing Palace Music and Charles Clay rubbed Estrapade while we had them back there for the Arlington Million. We were done training one morning. He was relaxed. I went into his stall to put a flake of alfalfa in the corner. That's when he wheeled around and measured me up. He looked at me over his shoulder, backed up two steps and started firing with his back feet. I was down on my hands and knees and literally dove out of the stall. He had me dead."

Hassinger escaped, and lived to tell the hairy tale. At the end

of 1986 Palace Music went on his merry way, and eventually
Hassinger joined the Paulson stable based in Southern California
as the number two man behind head trainer Richard Lundy. By
the time the crop of 1991 yearlings arrived at the terraced splen-
dor of Brookside West, Hassinger was in charge of a large string
of Paulson runners at the nearby San Luis Rey Downs training
center. Lundy spent a lot of his time on the road, commuting the
hundred miles between Bonsall and the Los Angeles racetracks
to the north, whenever a Paulson horse would run. Back at
Brookside, Hassinger would help hold down the fort.

The Bonsall facility was unique among California thoroughbred training grounds. No other owner imported so
many horses from out of state. Paulson had a scattering of
trainers at East Coast tracks and in Europe. But, at Bonsall,
he had committed most of his efforts toward establishing a
place where his best horses could prepare for the rich purses
of the California racing program. Paulson built a home at
Brookside West, a cluster of condos and cottages for guests,
and a helicopter pad high on the hill where he could land his
Sikorsky and take off at a moment's notice. The horses could
train all day long on the private, three-quarter-mile track
without interference from outside stables. The Brookside
employees had a quality of racetrack life second to none.

Cigar arrived at Brookside West just two weeks after the
dust had settled on the most exciting day in the brief and
splashy history of the Paulson thoroughbred empire. At
Churchill Downs, where the Breeders' Cup races were run on
November 2, 1991, Paulson's colors were carried to victory in

the $1-million Breeders' Cup Mile by Opening Verse, who shocked the crowd of 66,204 with his odds of 26-to-1. That was nothing, though, compared to the scene that transpired a half hour later when Paulson's little chestnut colt Arazi, fresh in from France, rocked the racing world with his five-length victory in the $1-million Breeders' Cup Juvenile.

Prior to the Breeders' Cup, Paulson had sold half of Arazi to Sheikh Mohammed, and together they let themselves dream sweet dreams of a Kentucky Derby victory the following spring. Opening Verse, who was trained by Lundy, returned to California, where he reigned as the star of the stable at Brookside West. The new kids from Kentucky had a tough act to follow.

Still, they were a grand bunch of babies, with the breeding, the looks and the disposition to whet any appetite.

"They did a fantastic job breaking those horses in Kentucky," Hassinger praised. "The horses that came from Ted Carr were as broke as you could break 'em. The colts were very spirited. They didn't have a racetrack on the farm back there, so when they went to the racetrack in California it was like a new playground for them. It was a little bit like a rodeo at first, but they all settled down."

From the beginning it was apparent to both Lundy and Hassinger that Cigar was not among the more precocious of the freshly-turned two-year-olds of 1992. Physically, Cigar had "great structure but lacked mass," to Hassinger's eye, with striking similarities to Palace Music from the saddle forward. But it would be awhile before the colt would be ready to run. Like father, like son, Palace Music did not make his first start until March of his three-year-old season.

"Palace Music was a real good horse at three but he might have been best when he was five," Hassinger pointed out. "So that was in the back of our minds when we looked at Cigar. As for the mare, well, we'd never trained anything out of Solar Slew before, so we didn't have a lot to go on there."

Cigar's early life at Brookside was filled with easy jogs in the arena and then on the training track. At the end of the morning, Cigar and a few of his fellow two-year-olds would get a quiet trail ride around the perimeter of the Brookside property, climbing up the hills of the back pastures and then down again to the main barn located in the center of the complex. Slowly, the new kids began to reveal their personalities to the Brookside staff. Soon, Cigar became a favorite. With Lee Ricci, he became the one.

Ricci had been working with two-year-olds, prepping them for market, before she joined the staff at Brookside West in 1987. As an assistant to Lundy and then later to Hassinger, Ricci accompanied the young horses to the track and helped supervise their care. Her domain was the middle barn, where the best of the crop and those closest to racing were stabled. Everyone on the crew would take a stab at which one of the newcomers would rise above the rest, but that year it was tough. Eliza? Corby? Stuka? Diazo? There were dozens of candidates.

"We treated them all like they were going to be good ones, which is what you have to do when you have that many well-bred horses," Ricci said. "But you couldn't help being attracted to Cigar. He was just such a good-looking horse. He was always very personable. And he was always one of the riders' favorites. They'd buy a bottle of orange soda and give him half the bottle. They'd give him mints, bananas, all kinds of treats. He was the kind of horse that was fun to be around. When you get a lot of horses like that, there will always be the ones that none of the exercise riders want to get on. Then there will be the horses everybody wants to ride. Everybody wanted to ride Cigar."

Dr. Steve Allday, the Brookside West veterinarian, liked to bring his two children on routine rounds and did not worry when they approached the son of Palace Music. Later on, daughter Kelly would often ask, "How's Cigar?" Allday's earliest impressions of Cigar meshed with the rest of the staff— this was a grand colt with an unlimited future.

"The first thing I can remember was remarking how big he was," Allday recalled. "He was a very big colt at the end of his yearling year. He was real long cannon-boned with a big body. You could tell he was going to be a fairly good-sized horse. The first thing we did was paint his knees and hocks. Then later, in the middle of his two-year-old year, he started popping a curb behind. That's when we freeze-fired him. I prefer it to pin-firing or a blister because those procedures create so much scar tissue in a joint that sometimes you end up with a problem, unrelated to the original problem, caused by a treatment you did. With cryotherapy there was no invasive process to the joint. There's just the cryo unit and conductive gel to freeze the surface topically. The colt responded real well. He was back training in two or three days." The hair below Cigar's hock grew back white at the contact points of the cryo unit, leaving the leg with a grid pattern that looked as if the joint had been lightly singed by a waffle iron.

In the spring of the year, Paulson divided his two-year-olds among several Southern California trainers, including Gary Jones, Bill Shoemaker, Ron McAnally, Darrell Vienna and John Sadler. "I think it's a good idea," Paulson said at the time. "These are all top trainers. And with so many two-year-olds, this is a chance to keep them out of each other's way. Each trainer will have their special group." The bulk of the two-year-olds, however, stayed with Lundy at Brookside West. Among them were Eliza and Cigar. Lundy felt that Eliza was the most precocious of the bunch. And Cigar, while physically immature, had potential to burn.

The normally tranquil atmosphere of Brookside West was shattered in July of 1992 when Paulson fired Richard Lundy. In an attempt to preserve some continuity, Paulson told Hassinger he was temporarily in charge. After getting over the shellshock, Hassinger plunged into his new role with the determination of a man intent to make the most of an incredible stroke of luck. Twenty-nine at the time, Hassinger was a New Jersey native who had been around horses most of his life. His maternal uncle was John R. Gaines, founder of the Breeders' Cup and one of Kentucky's top breeders. Hassinger worked at Gainesway Farm in Lexington before heading west to work as a groom for Whittingham and then as an assistant to Richard Cross, who trained a few horses for Paulson. When Paulson hired Lundy—also a Whittingham disciple—Lundy was swamped with applications for the number two slot. Hassinger fit the bill.

When Lundy left, however, Hassinger first assumed he would be part of an overall house cleaning. Instead, Paulson decided to keep Hassinger as his primary California trainer, while continuing to entrust a portion of the stable to other local trainers.

Lightning struck quickly for Paulson and his freshly-minted trainer. Eliza blossomed into a champion during the last part of 1992. Fowda, a four-year-old daughter of Strawberry Road, won the prestigious Spinster Stakes at Keeneland, beating champion Paseana in the process. With each major victory Hassinger's confidence grew, while the steady stream of quality Brookside horses supplied their own momentum. No sooner did Hassinger return from Eliza's Breeders' Cup victory at Gulfstream Park on October 31, 1992, than he was faced with a new batch of yearlings from Kentucky and the remnants of the previous class—among them Cigar—who had yet to begin their careers.

As 1992 came to an end, Cigar was stabled at the San Luis Rey Downs training center, a few miles down the road from Brookside West. His workouts were getting faster, pointing more toward racing readiness than simple condition. On January 22, 1993, Cigar worked a fast half mile in forty-six seconds. Thirteen days later he worked five-eighths of a mile in a minute and two seconds. On February 13, he went three-quarters of a mile in a minute and twelve seconds—true racehorse time. "He was doing everything right, like a good horse. It was time to try him," Hassinger recalled. On February 17, Hassinger sent Cigar to the San Luis Rey Downs starting gate and gave the exercise rider instructions for a three-furlong work to put the colt on edge for a race the following weekend. Cigar responded with a clocking that shaded thirty-four seconds. Three days later Cigar walked onto a horse van and headed for the big city.

It rained that week in Southern California. Nothing unusual about that. February is usually the state's wettest month. The racetrack at Santa Anita was packed tight to prevent the penetration of too much moisture, but the surface was still muddy enough to bother an inexperienced racehorse. When thirteen of those inexperienced three-year-old colts entered the race Hassinger had in mind, Cigar was placed on the "also-eligible" list. Sort of like waiting for a table. Four horses were withdrawn from the race, however, and Cigar was seated with no trouble.

And so it was that Cigar made his competitive debut on a cool, cloudy Sunday, February 21, 1993, at Santa Anita Park, where Palace Music had lost that heartbreaker in the Breeders' Cup Mile six and a half years earlier. The distance was three-quarters of a mile for a purse of $28,000. The track was muddy but drying out. And of the eight other non-winners in the field Cigar was the only one trained at San Luis Rey. He went to the gate, calm but curious, and entered stall number nine on the extreme outside. The start was good, but after that things got confusing. Cigar raced wide down the backstretch, flanking a cluster of horses in the middle of the pack. After about a half mile it just wasn't fun anymore. His jockey, Patrick Valenzuela, showed mercy and let Cigar slow down gradually while absorbing the new sights. Cigar finished seventh that day, officially beaten thirteen lengths by the winner, named Demigod, a colt trained by Richard Mandella.

There was nothing to be discouraged about. Hassinger came from the Charlie Whittingham school of training, and Whittingham was notorious for using early races as learning tools. Many young horses need a race or two before they figure out how to be competitive. As creatures of habit, most thoroughbreds are wary of new experiences. After one or two races, they grow more accustomed to the crowd, the noise, and the intensity of the competitive situation—jockeys screaming at each other and their own mounts, whips smacking horseflesh, an announcer screaming in the distance. Some horses understand from the start. Many horses never learn.

Cigar returned to San Luis Rey Downs and picked up where he left off. Hassinger decided to wait for the weather to break and the Hollywood Park season to open in late April before running Cigar again. In the meantime, the colt continued to give his trainer good vibes. On April 25, Cigar worked five furlongs in just over a minute. On the morning of April 30, he gave Hassinger chills with a six-furlong workout that took barely a minute and eleven seconds. Cigar did not need to run much faster than that to win a race.

The next day was Derby Day in America. Saturday, May 1, and the Paulsons were at Churchill Downs to watch two of their Brookside babies run in the world's most famous horse race. Allen Paulson's single-minded goal to win the Kentucky Derby was no secret to his friends and family. He could still taste the disappointment of 1992, when Arazi came to the Derby with all the fanfare of Lafayette, only to finish a tired, disoriented eighth. Prior to that, Paulson's colors had been carried by Vernon Castle in the 1986 Derby, but he finished fifteenth, beating just one horse. This time around Paulson had two chances in a Derby that was considered a wide open affair. Diazo was trained by Bill Shoemaker and Corby was in the hands of John Sadler. What both colts lacked in experience they made up for in raw ability. Corby pressed the pace and was fighting for the lead at the top of the long stretch before fading to finish sixth, while Diazo came on fast at the end to finish fifth, right alongside his Brookside classmate.

Eight days later, on Sunday, May 9, Cigar reappeared in a six-furlong maiden race at Hollywood Park. This was more like it. Cigar was distracted at the break and let his five opponents get the jump. But soon he was in the thick of the race. He pulled Valenzuela to the lead as the field approached the far turn and then, in an impressive display of speed, he opened up quickly and turned the show into a one-horse race. At the end, Cigar was cruising along two and a quarter lengths ahead of the second horse, Golden Slewpy. His official time as he glided past the finish line was one minute, nine and two-fifths seconds.

Cigar's first win created barely a ripple in the wider racing world. From the crowded herd of more than three thousand horses in training around Southern California, he had become just another maiden race winner. Essentially, Hassinger and the Paulsons had on their hands an unstable weapon of powerful potential. They toyed with various scenarios—including a full throttle plan to stay on the dirt and aim for the $200,000 Swaps Stakes at the end of July. But because Cigar's shins and hocks still were subject to stress and his knees sometimes carried a degree of suspicious heat, Hassinger had to tread a fine line in his training and racing strategy as he looked to the future— both immediate and distant. So, in consultation with the Paulsons and their veterinary advisors, Hassinger made a decision that has been second-guessed more than any in the modern history of the sport. For the time being, he would race Cigar on the grass.

Through the distorted lens of historical hindsight, Cigar's early career spent racing exclusively on grass sticks out like a thorn among the roses of his sixteen-race winning streak, since all of the streak was accomplished on the dirt. One-for-eleven on the grass followed by sixteen straight on the dirt? What could they have been thinking? As it turns out, they were thinking of the horse.

"The decision to keep him on the turf was a lot broader picture than what people might think," Hassinger explained. "Yes, his father was a grass horse. Palace Music came to America a grass horse and Whittingham kept him on the grass. But Charlie never tried him on the dirt because of his knees. It would have been too tough on him. Cigar was much more correct than his sire. He was just physically immature. It was taking awhile for his bones to get strong and his knees to set. I'm convinced that it is not the training and the surfaces that breaks down horses. It is asking them for too much when they are still physically immature.

"I don't train racehorses—and I didn't train Cigar—to win the next race. Each race in the career of a young horse should be designed to set him up to improve. I was lucky to learn from good people that you train for the next year or two or three down the road. You plan programs for horses. Cigar's program was to put him on the grass initially to keep him around longer. I didn't think it was a fluke the way he broke his maiden. Putting him on the dirt later on would have always been an option, as far as I was concerned. Keeping him as sound as possible early was the only way he was going to get there."

Hassinger was able to economically justify his strategy for Cigar by pointing to the rich array of grass races offered exclusively for three-year-olds that filled the last half of the 1993 California stakes calendar. There were hundreds of thousands of dollars up for grabs, with the $400,000 Hollywood Derby culminating the series in November. Fresh from his maiden win, Cigar commenced his grass racing career on May 23 at Hollywood Park in a mile and one-sixteenth race worth $39,000. He took a clear lead late in the race, but his inexperience did him in. Alone in front, his mind wandered and his cadence slowed. Three horses took advantage of Cigar's lapse and passed him late. He finished fourth, although he was beaten less than two lengths.

Hassinger liked what he saw. Cigar ran well enough to deserve another crack at decent grass competition. On June 12, while most of the attention was focused on the champion mare Paseana in the featured Milady Handicap, Cigar took on a quality allowance field at a mile and one-sixteenth on the Hollywood grass. This time he finished third, a finish that grew more respectable with the future accomplishments of the horses who were first and second: Nonproductiveasset and Tossofthecoin. At least, compared to them, Cigar's name sounded better.

The high-wire act continued. Cigar's maturing legs remained a concern to Hassinger and the Paulson staff. No radical measures were taken in his veterinary care. But it was clear the big colt could not be campaigned with fearless abandon. As the racing circuit moved south in the summer of 1993, Cigar would have a soft, more forgiving grass course over which to compete at Del Mar. On the afternoon of August 18, with Chris McCarron riding him for the first time, Cigar responded with a thoroughly professional victory in a $36,000 allowance race and brought the crowd along for the ride. For the first time in his life, Cigar was the betting favorite.

That was the good news. Between races, Hassinger and his crew had to deal with the bad.

"His knees started flaring up at Del Mar," Hassinger recalled. "He really didn't like training on the dirt course there, so we tried to work him on the grass as much as possible. Again, that's the immaturity we were facing with him all along."

Hassinger resisted the temptation to try Cigar in the Del Mar Derby, with its $300,000 prize, scheduled that summer for September 6. Instead, he finessed one more Del Mar start out of the colt on September 3 in a one-mile allowance event. It was a good race, probably the best he had ever run, even though he finished second to Kingdom of Spain. Cigar was beaten half a length.

McCarron was disappointed. The jockey thought Cigar would continue to improve after his August form and take the race by storm. For his part, Hassinger merely added the September race to the larger puzzle and planned for the next step. It was time Cigar tried stakes company. The target was the Ascot Handicap at Bay Meadows, just south of San Francisco, on September 25.

Bay Meadows liked to celebrate its Ascot Day with a taste of British pomp and tradition. Ladies dressed to kill and their gentlemen donned formal wear and top hats. Hospitality tents offered smoked salmon, strawberries and champagne. The local Rolls Royce and Bentley clubs convened at the track for the day, parking their collector cars in the infield. Their proud owners feasted from gourmet picnic baskets and invited admirers to study their reflections in the glossy fenders.

Hassinger was cautiously optimistic as Cigar went postward that day against ten opponents. Among them was Nonproductiveasset, the mouthful from Hollywood Park, and Siebe, a son of Dahar who was bred by Paulson in Kentucky and schooled there by Mac Carr, just like Cigar. When he raced at age two, Siebe was claimed for $40,000 and took up residence at the stable of trainer Frank Olivares. But the magic of that 1990 Paulson crop went with him. By the time he ran in the Ascot, Siebe already was a stakes winner.

The race unfolded perfectly for Cigar. With Valenzuela back in the saddle, he galloped along just behind the early pace, gracefully moved into contention on the final turn, and then took the lead when the pacesetter, Wild Gold, blew the turn and carried several horses far afield. By the time Cigar reached the furlong pole, with an eighth of a mile to run, he was all alone at the head of the pack. To Hassinger, he never looked more beautiful. Reaching out with his long strides, his blaze flickering into view as he thrust his elegant head ever forward, Cigar was at long last running as he had been born to run. Then Hassinger glanced to his left. The spell was broken.

From out of the field, first Siebe and then Nonproductiveasset shook loose and came tumbling through the long grass down the middle of the Bay Meadows stretch. At the same time, Cigar's stride began to lose some of its length. Hassinger fought back the rising tide of nausea in the pit of his stomach as he watched the two pursuers bear down on the big colt. They reached Cigar with less than a hundred yards to run. Cigar, his momentum lost, tried to fight back but could not. The finish line arrived and the three swept past the post together, with Cigar's long, graying tail trailing behind. Siebe, nearest the stands, won by a neck over Nonproductiveasset, who in turn finished a head in front of Cigar.

"To me, that was his most disappointing race, and not just because he got beat by a horse Mr. Paulson used to own," Hassinger said. "I thought he should have won. And turning for home he really looked like a winner. Then his inexperience caught up with him. He got to the front and he was all alone. That was it. He thought he'd won. He was still learning."

Hassinger had no reason to back off. The next California stop for three-year-olds on the grass came at Santa Anita Park in the Volante Handicap on November 5. Since it was being run on the eve of the Breeders' Cup, the Volante had an unusually critical audience of international horsemen and media. Cigar once again ran well without winning. He finished second, two lengths behind Eastern Memories and ahead of Tinners Way, Jeune Homme and Bon Point, all budding stakes stars. Bill Mott was at Santa Anita that day, but he missed the race. Mott was back at the barns, tending to his Breeders' Cup starters. Among them was Madeleine Paulson's Fraise, the defending champion in the Breeders' Cup Turf. Mott took note of the Volante results, but Cigar made no particular impression. He was just another horse, trained by somebody else.

Cigar's performance in the Volante was good enough to justify a try in the Hollywood Derby. It was the last stop for the cream of the three-year-old California grass horses before they turned four and were forced to compete against older, more experienced veterans. The Paulsons were not alone. As they stood beneath the trees of the vast Hollywood Park saddling paddock, near the monument marking the grave of the great Native Diver, they were surrounded by the owners, trainers and handlers of thirteen other horses trying for that one last brass ring of 1993. Lost in the crowd of his first appearance in a top-class, Grade I event, Cigar's modest accomplishments were virtually ignored by the betting public. His odds were a soaring 24-to-1.

At that point, though, the Paulsons were immune to such petty slights. Their week had begun in the depths of despair with the loss of Capel, another of their golden babies from the crop of 1990. Trained by Gary Jones, Capel fractured both forelegs while running in a grass race at Santa Anita on November 13. There was very little choice in the face of such extreme damage. An attending veterinarian said he had never seen such combination of injuries before. The legs were beyond repair. Capel had to be euthanized.

The experience left the Paulsons on edge as they watched Cigar saddle up for the Hollywood Derby. His white-rimmed left eye surveyed the scene around him as he picked up vibes from such familiar faces as Eastern Memories, Jeune Homme, Bon Point and Nonproductiveasset. With such a large field, the race itself was a cavalry charge. Valenzuela tried to save what ground he could while letting Cigar run freely on the outside. Entering the final turn, with three of the nine furlongs left to run, Cigar was cruising along just behind the leaders, Eastern Memories and Explosive Red. But then, as the field straightened away into the close-cropped Hollywood stretch, Valenzuela felt Cigar weaken. His stride lost its smooth, effortless rhythm and he began to lose position. As horses swirled around him, Valenzuela took a controlling hold of the reins and guided the big colt through the final furlong of another disappointing race. Cigar finished eleventh...but at least he finished.

On the distant turn, far from the excitement of the finish line, the Irish colt Fatherland had been pulled to a stop long before Explosive Red took the lead and went on to win. Fatherland had shattered the pastern of his left foreleg, one of the bones linking the ankle to the hoof. The only thing that could have saved him was complicated surgery and a long, miserable period of recovery with no promise of success. His anguished owners, Robert and Beverly Lewis, sadly agreed to let the colt be euthanized.

And Cigar? It was his knees, those immature knees, that came out of the Hollywood Derby needing attention. The Paulsons breathed a sigh of relief. Cigar's condition was common, and the solution was routine. The decision was made to perform arthroscopic surgery to remove what appeared to be small chips above the second, or intermediate carpal bones of both knees. The chips were hardly visible on X-ray. But their continued presence created an irritation to the joints that would become chronic if not removed. In many cases, such minor joint problems in racehorses are treated by regular injections of a corticosteroid compound that can reduce the affect of a chip. Injections, though less expensive than arthroscopic surgery, can also debilitate the joint structure over a period of time. The Paulsons were not interested in shortcuts with Cigar.

Two weeks after the Hollywood Derby, Cigar was led into

the anesthesia chamber of the Helen Woodward Animal Center Equine Clinic, just a few miles east of Del Mar racetrack. The colt had spent the night before at the clinic in a large, airy stall. Early on the morning of December 4 he was given a mild sedative to quell any nervous fears. Once the anesthetic began to take hold, a little after eight o'clock, Cigar was gently eased to the floor with the help of a specially designed, hinged guide wall. His airway was intubated, his legs were wrapped in padding and he was hoisted, upside down, along a track that led into the adjacent operating room. Dr. Lynn Richardson was in command. His anesthetist was Dr. Robert "Rusty" Mills. Standing in a corner of the operating room, eyes glued to their baby, were Allen and Madeleine Paulson.

Cigar was lowered onto the blue tarp of the contoured operating table and secured, legs in the air. His knees were shaved and scrubbed. Working on the right knee first, Dr. Richardson inserted an arthroscope—with a tiny television camera attached—into one side of the joint. Then, from the other side, he introduced a delicate scraping tool and began to "clean up" the irregular surface of the bone. The Paulsons were able to view the inside of the joint and the tools at work on the screen of a video monitor set up next to Richardson.

"How does it look?" Madeleine said. "Is it bad?"

"Actually, not bad at all," Richardson replied. "No real surprises. There's the chip. Not very big."

The whole thing—both knees—took Richardson fifty minutes. Cigar was hoisted into a recovery room, where

Richardson and an assistant maintained a quiet vigil while the colt emerged from the anesthetic. Less than an hour later, Cigar was on his feet, still a bit groggy, and walking down the path to his stall. After two days of observation and fresh bandages, the colt was back on a van, heading home to Brookside West. In his follow-up letter to Hassinger, Richardson prescribed a regimen of post-operative care and predicted, with reasonable assurance, "This horse should have a good prognosis for return to racing form in a relatively short time."

About a year later, in late November of 1994, Steve Allday stuck his head into Richardson's office at the Helen Woodward Clinic to pay his respects.

"By the way," Allday added, "that horse you operated on last year has won a couple of nice races back in New York."

Richardson looked up. No particular horse came to mind. "Which one was that?" he wondered.

"You know," Allday replied. "That big, good-looking colt of the Paulsons. You went into his knees. Remember Cigar?"

CHAPTER 4

HEARTLAND

Jim Bayes was trying to nail the shoes on a fidgety colt standing in the shedrow of the Jack Van Berg barn in Omaha. He would have been done a long time ago, he figured, if the kid all dressed up like an exercise rider and holding the shank could just get his act together long enough to keep the darn horse quiet. Bent over double, Bayes finally got tired wrestling with the colt's back leg and barked, "What's the matter, you green s.o.b.? Don't you even know how to hold a horse?"

The kid saw red. His pale eyes went hard. "Hold him yourself!" he barked as he tossed away the lead and stomped off. "I don't even work here." Bayes just shook his head, hollered for a groom to come help, and finished the job. "Good riddance," he thought. "Smart-mouthed kid."

It was the early 1970s, at Ak-Sar-Ben racetrack, and the Van Berg stable was the center of the Midwestern racing universe. All the action was at Jack's barn. Owners lined up to fill the stalls. Rival trainers were helpless to stop those purple and gold colors. Young riders flocked there, from the Rockies to the bayou, just to beg for jobs.

One of the young pilgrims was that exercise rider—who also happened to be the man who someday would train Cigar. William I. Mott, of the Mobridge, South Dakota, Motts, was fresh out of high school and hungry for a taste of the world.

He was anxious to test the lessons he had learned at the side of such horsemen as Ray Goehring, Keith Asmussen and his father, Dr. Tom Mott, better known as "The Flying Veterinarian." He was ready to get on with the life he had chosen for as long as he could remember.

Bill Mott was a baby-faced former high school wrestler and football player, with blond sideburns poking out below his helmet and a cocksure attitude bubbling just beneath his placid, Nordic exterior. When he landed a spot full time with Van Berg, Jim Bayes—farrier extraordinaire—started cutting young Mott some slack. He discovered a kid who was willing to work twice as hard as the next guy. Mott tried to make every minute count. Bayes took Mott under his wing and watched him grow until, one day, the student became the master.

The trainer of Cigar was the third of three boys born to Thomas and Olive Mott. They grew up in a roomy farmhouse discovered by Tom Mott in another town and transplanted to 1018 Eighth Avenue West in Mobridge proper. Tom Mott's clinic, with thirty acres of pens and pasture, was located about a mile down the road. The oldest boy, Donovan, was born in 1947 and named for an uncle killed over France in World War II. Robert came along in 1949, and then came Bill, on July 29, 1953. The smallest of the three brothers, Bill later would complain that Don and Rob ate faster and more often. Little wonder they flew past six feet tall to leave their kid brother in the dust.

There were maybe five thousand people in Mobridge at the time. Located twenty-five miles due south of the North Dakota state line, deep in the heart of cattle and farm country, the town sat on the eastern side of a ninety-degree northward bend in the wide Missouri River. Mobridge was known for its livestock auction and its hospital. Across the river, the Standing Rock Sioux Indian Reservation spread to the north and the west, while the Cheyenne River Reservation bordered to the southwest. Modern Mobridge is a fisherman's paradise, hosting tournaments and regional tourists.

At the height of his practice in the 1960s, Tom Mott's business was spread out the length and breadth of the territory. All three boys put in time driving their father to medical emergencies far and wide. Sometimes Tom Mott would pull twenty-four hour shifts just to accommodate his caseload. When he couldn't make it to a farm in his pick-up truck he would take off in his Piper Super Cub and land in an empty field. Tom Mott logged more than a thousand trips. Everybody relied on Tom Mott.

The three Mott boys eventually veered off in their own directions. Don, a superb athlete, headed for California after high school graduation and was later drafted into the Army. He was wounded in Vietnam. Rob acquired his father's taste for flying. As young as fourteen he would sometimes "borrow" the plane, hop down the road to visit some friends, then refill the gas tank to the old mark once he got home.

Bill was bitten by a love for the animals. Working with his father, he got to know horses inside and out. Tom Mott cleared a pasture at the clinic, built his son a small training track, and spent $320 to buy Bill an honest-to-goodness racemare named My Assets. Bill galloped her, rubbed her, and drove her the hundred miles south to Fort Pierre, where William Irving Mott saddled his first winner at age fifteen.

Ray Goehring was not the least bit surprised. Goehring, who traded in horses and cattle, got to know the Motts when he ran the livestock auction barn in McLaughlin, thirty miles northwest of Mobridge. Tom Mott was the auction vet.

"I did some wrestling myself when I was younger, so I'd go to some of Bill's matches when he was a sophomore in high school," Goehring said. "He was pretty good. But I don't think his heart and soul was in it. Not quite like he was into horses. That's all we ever did was talk horses. When I gave him a summer job we had eighteen or twenty horses. It wasn't long before I'd put him in command when I went home on weekends, for the simple reason he liked what he was doing and knew what he was doing. He was in command over people who were twice his age. Bill would sooner go without a meal than cut his horses short. When he started training that mare My Assets we even challenged each other a couple times. If I remember right, he beat me once and I beat him once.

"Bill learned that everybody gets to know a horse in a different way, and that every horse is different," Goehring went on. "When he worked for me we had one that wanted to run with long feet. I'd run him, he'd win, and a guy would come along and buy him. They'd shorten up his feet and they could not get him to run. They asked if I wanted to buy the horse back. So I did. We let his feet grow for awhile and won with him again. Sold him three times that summer!"

Mott and Goehring raced their horses in places like Aberdeen, Park Jefferson and Fort Pierre in those distant, late '60s summers. Mott remembers the rites of passage: the betting coups, the cowboy bars, and cadging beers when he was still underage. "My dad over there"—he'd point to Ray —"said it was okay." Goehring was the leading trainer on the circuit, so it was definitely okay, since the bartender probably cashed on one of his horses earlier that same day.

"We'd always have peppermint schnapps on ice at the barn," Mott said. "A drink of that between races sure tasted good on those hot summer days."

"Yeah," Goehring laughed. "We did a lot of training on that peppermint schnapps. And nobody worked harder than we did."

Mott graduated from Ray Goehring to the larger operation run by Keith Asmussen down the road in the tiny town of Agar, population ninety-eight. "About twenty of 'em were Asmussens," said Keith, who fathered champion rider Cash Asmussen. "I had eighty horses, a lot of them quarter horses. We raced all over South Dakota, Nebraska, Colorado. Bill worked as hard as you could work, and he had to love it for what I was paying him. I think it was about two hundred and fifty dollars a month. Yes, I said a month."

After high school Mott was anxious to dive headlong into the business. He went from Omaha to Detroit, where he cashed in on his Van Berg connection and went to work for Bob Irwin, a disciple of Jack Van Berg's legendary father, Marion. In 1974, Mott rejoined Jack's Omaha stable and showed enough ability to earn a shot as an assistant trainer. Two years later, they made history.

Jack Van Berg was a larger-than-life Nebraska farm boy version of John Wayne who would laugh with you, slap you on the back, and never expect you to work harder than he did—which was pretty much all the time. His successful operation naturally drew talented people, and Van Berg knew enough to sift through the various personalities to let the best rise to the top. Van Berg had horses at racetracks from coast to coast, but they did the most damage through the country's mid-section. The tireless Van Berg would hop from Omaha to Chicago to Louisiana to Hot Springs to Kentucky to Detroit—like Henry Kissinger on a peace mission—touching base constantly with each of his many strings. If necessary Jack would strap on his blacksmith apron and work on problem feet, then leave town in a cloud of dust.

Mostly, though, Van Berg let his top assistants do their thing. That's how Mott learned to operate in the big time. During that incredible 1976 season, with Van Berg as ringmaster, the stable won four hundred and ninety-six races and purses totaling $2.9 million. Both numbers set North American records by a country mile. Van Berg had the young Frank Brothers in charge of the horses in Louisiana and Kentucky, while Mott did most of his winning in Michigan and Illinois. Both assistants used the Van Berg connection as a springboard to careers on their own. As Mott went on to build a following in Kentucky and Chicago, Brothers became one of the all-time leading trainers on the Louisiana circuit. In 1991,

Brothers won both the Preakness and Belmont Stakes with the champion three-year-old colt Hansel.

Mott cut loose from Van Berg in the fall of 1978. He headed south to Florida—where he finished third in the Widener Handicap with the converted claimer Singleton—then settled in for the springtime meet at Hazel Park, up in the fingers of the Michigan mitt. The riches and prestige of Belmont Park were somewhere in a different universe. As far as Mott was concerned, he was already playing the big room.

"When I was growing up, Omaha was like the ultimate place to be racing," Mott said. "Then I found myself at places like Detroit and Hazel Park. I didn't think it could get any better. That's where my horses belonged, and I guess as far as I was concerned, that's where I belonged, too."

Mott got a reputation as a cold-eyed claiming whiz who kept his cards close to his vest and was not afraid to bet his money. He tried to mix in a few allowance and stakes horses in the stable, but his name was made as a man who could find run in a claimer where other trainers could not. In the fall of 1981, after establishing a beachhead in Kentucky, Mott finished in a tie for the training titles at Keeneland and Churchill Downs. In the spring of 1982 he won the title at Churchill Downs, and did it again in the spring of 1983 and '84. Eventually, he racked up enough wins to become the leading trainer in the history of Churchill Downs.

Mott broke through in 1984 with a pair of headline stakes horses. Taylor's Special, a colt bred to peak at about six furlongs, won the Louisiana Derby and then took the

Blue Grass Stakes to give Mott a shot at the Kentucky Derby. Heatherten, a gray mare who was already a proven commodity, jumped up a notch for Mott and took him all the way to Belmont Park, where she won the Hempstead Handicap in the spring and the Ruffian Handicap in the fall.

That he could handle without batting an eye. It was running a horse in the Kentucky Derby for the first time that tested Mott's thirty-year-old maturity. He was accustomed to the flood of visitors and swarming mass of media filling the Churchill Downs backstretch leading up to the race each May. But he was always on the outside looking in. The Mott barn was easy to spot, with the brown "M" resting between two stripes on the yellow webbings and saddlecloths. Until Taylor's Special came along, however, there was no real threat from the intense Derby crush.

Tom Mott and Jim Bayes—Bill's brain trust—were on the scene watching Mott go through his baptism of Derby fire. As the local star with the Blue Grass winner, he was almost as popular as the prime rib at Pat's Steak House. The interviews were almost nonstop, and Mott held his own in terms of column inches with those seasoned veterans of Derby verbiage, Woody Stephens and D. Wayne Lukas. Even Jack Van Berg had one in the race, as did Richard Mandella, who crept into town late Derby week with a longshot that did not belong.

One morning, as the Derby neared and nerves were starting to fray, Dr. Mott and Bayes had a ringside seat when a long, black Lincoln limousine pulled up at the Mott barn and disgorged none other than Howard Cosell. The famous

Mouth of radio and TV was there to bestow upon Mott an audience in advance of the ABC television coverage.

"Watch this," Bayes said with a chuckle as Bill caught sight of the limo. It was blocking the path leading out of the shedrow, and Mott had a set ready to head for the track.

"What in hell do you think you're doing?" Mott yelled at the limo driver. "Get that thing the hell out of the way! How're we supposed to get the horses out of the barn?"

Bayes just shook his head. He had seen it before. "Can you believe that silly sonofagun? His one chance for an interview on national TV and he blows it by chasing away Howard Cosell!"

Such occasional bursts of youthful excess were at odds with Mott's normally serene demeanor. Under most circumstances he was mellow and deliberate. Ask Mott a question and he would usually take it under advisement for an unpredictable period of time. After the wheels have turned for awhile, he'd furrow his brow, press his lips together, and make like he is about to launch into the State of the Union address.

"Welllll..."

Then there will be another long pause, and the phone will ring, a horse will walk by, or someone will drop in and distract him from the topic immediately at hand. Those not familiar with the pace of the man will give up and figure the moment has passed. Better luck next time. If they leave, they lose, because Mott has not forgotten where he was or what he was going to say. Those who do business with Mott have learned to hang tough. A half-hour after the fact he may call up the question—as if it had been standing in a long bank line waiting its turn—and deliver an answer with patience and precision. Many times people forgot what they asked in the first place.

Such behavior is no surprise to those who know where Mott grew up. The Dakota plains and Midwestern vistas leave a lot of room for solitary thought, especially when a young man spends as much time with animals as he does with people. Towns are small, weather can be fierce, and reasons to talk are sometimes few and far between. Stir in the natural reticence of his Scandinavian heritage, and Mott could seem downright chilly at times.

"Midwesterners are a little bit different," said Hall of Fame trainer John Nerud, who was born in Minatare, Nebraska, a dot on the map even smaller than Mobridge. "We're hayshakers, and a little bit slow. People out there have a greater tendency to be honest. When you come out of that country you've got a lot to learn. Out there, if a man said he'd be over and help you Thursday, he'd be there unless he was sick or dead. You never thought anything about it. You were a man of your word if you were a man."

Nerud met Mott in the fall of 1990 at Belmont Park when Kentucky Derby winner Unbridled, trained by Carl Nafzger, was temporarily stabled in Mott's barn. As manager of the Frances Genter stable, Nerud had planned the breeding of Unbridled and raised him as a foal. He took a look around Mott's operation and liked what he saw. The next year Nerud asked Mott to train a few of his own horses.

"Training is secondary to taking care of horses, and Bill is a good caretaker," Nerud said. "He comes out of the same district I did, and we had to make a living with our horses. That's when you find out if a guy can train. Put up his own money and train 'em."

It did not take Ted Carr long to get a handle on Mott either, once they met through the Paulson horses raised at Brookside Farm in Kentucky.

"He's a cowboy type," Carr said. "A hands-on horseman. To me that separates the real top horseman—the guy who can do things with a horse. What to do, when to do, how to do. *Why* to do."

Ray Goehring boiled the Mott style down even further. "Patience and time. Time and patience. That's why Bill is so successful with older horses like Cigar. The good ones need time, and Bill gives it to them."

On the walls of Mott's office of Belmont barn 25, by the end of the 1995 campaign, there were five photographs of Cigar, four pictures of South Dakota, and a framed print of a cowboy and his pony entitled "Chores Come Hell or High Water." A storebought greeting card sitting on a corner file cabinet was made for "Daddy," only the "dy" had been crossed out. Inside, the inscription read, "Dear Dad, You are the best, most wonderful dad in the world. No dad could be better than you. Love, Brady."

It was one o'clock in the afternoon, and Mott was finally through calling his clients. He pushed back from his desk, grabbed a broom from the corner and started sweeping the linoleum floor.

"I know it seems kind of pointless," he said as he swept. "Trying to sweep up a barn. I could be doing this all morning long if I wanted to. Given the chance, I'm afraid I'd really be kind of a neat freak. But working around a stable, you have to make certain concessions."

It was library quiet out in the shedrow now that most of the work was done for the day. But quiet is the way Mott liked to train. Even at the peak of morning activity, when sets of horses were going in and out and more were on the wash racks, the sounds were muted: there was soft Spanish, crunching gravel, running water, the occasional "Let's go!" from Mott or one of the assistants. If a horse kicked the side of his stall, everybody heard it. If a horse coughed or even cleared his throat, everybody heard. The loudest noise was the phone. Mott usually kept it on one ring, then the answering machine would kick in.

"I like the horses to relax, and the only time you can relax is when it's quiet," Mott said. "It's the same with me. People start talking loud in the barn, even if they're laughing, I don't really like it."

Whether he would admit it or not, Mott had recreated in his stables the family atmosphere of his youth. He functioned best under such circumstances, when turmoil was at a minimum and the work at hand was paramount. He made sure everyone gained satisfaction from a job well done. He was honest in his praise as he was diligent in a reprimand for a mistake that simply should not have been made. He spent most of his life at the track, anyway, from five-thirty in the morning to well past noon, and then back again for the late afternoon feeding until there was nothing more for him to do.

Away from the track, in the years right after leaving Van Berg, Mott maintained a relationship with a co-worker who exercised horses and wanted to train on her own. The relationship ended badly in 1984, but as it turned out, the timing could not have been better. About a thousand miles away, up in Vermont, Tina Kotowiecz had just split with her boyfriend as well.

They were already related, sort of. Tina's sister Lynn was married to Terry Mason, one of Mott's assistant trainers. Lynn encouraged Tina to visit Louisville and get together with Bill. Tina wasn't interested. At least not right away.

"I was still hurt, but finally I said yes, and I flew to Detroit where Bill was running some horses. He came up from Kentucky. The date lasted about a week and a half. I went with him to Toronto to buy horses, then back to Louisville, then to Louisiana to run a horse, then back to Kentucky and back to Detroit. I didn't know anything about racing. They were talking a language that I didn't understand. But it was all pretty exciting."

For Mott, Tina was just what the doctor ordered.

"I think the fact that she didn't know horse racing was maybe what I was looking for," he said. "I'd been with someone who was as involved with it as I was, and it was like you could never get away from it even when you might want to. With Tina, I actually had some conversations about things like current events. Although I might not have done much of the talking."

They were married in Louisville on June 30, 1985, in a wedding complete with horse drawn carriage. Tina had fallen in love, not only with Bill, but with the people she was meeting because of him. Coming from a suburban Massachusetts town, she felt at peace with the country feel of the racetrack community. As she learned the business, and as Mott's business grew, Tina began to handle the stable books, billings and correspondence. In 1985, their first year together, the Mott runners soared to earnings of $3.4 million, best of his budding career. The books never looked better.

At the end of 1986, Mott was offered the position of private trainer for the New York stable of Bert and Diana Firestone. Their horses were world renowned. The Firestones had won the 1980 Kentucky Derby with Genuine Risk and a 1982 North American championship with the willowy Irish filly April Run. Mott weighed the advantages of a set salary and simplified lifestyle against the risk of putting all his eggs into one basket. He took the job, which commenced that December. The Motts celebrated by conceiving their first child.

By the following August, Tina was close to delivery. She spent a week settling Bill into their Saratoga rental, then headed back home to Long Island. Bill planned to follow when the date drew nearer. On the way downstate, the car carrying Tina and a friend broke down. They were towed to a diner, then hitched a ride with a horse van. That did not last long. The bounce of the hydraulic seats, combined with a rain-soaked highway full of potholes, made her think labor was near. By the time they got to a tollbooth, Tina had gone far enough. The driver told the toll collector he had a pregnant woman on board who had to get out. The word spread like wildfire from booth to booth. Soon, everyone wanted to know about the woman in labor. "I am not in labor!" Tina yelled out the window of the van. "I just need a cab!"

The baby didn't budge. A week and a half later, on August 23, 1987, Brady Thomas Mott was born after thirty-two hours of labor. To mark Brady's welcome into the world, Mott tossed up a personal best season of stable earnings with a total of just over $4 million. The only names above him were Lukas, Whittingham, Van Berg and Stephens.

Through the next several years, the cycle of life and death visited the Mott household with momentous regularity. Olive Mott died in 1990 at the age of seventy. On December 26, 1991, Tina gave birth to Riley Mott, this time without the benefit of a van ride. Dr. Tom Mott, in failing health since the death of his wife, was at the hospital for the arrival of his Christmas grandson.

"That was important," recalled Bill. "I'm glad my dad was able to see Riley, and spend some time with Brady. After my mom died he was going downhill pretty fast, and he didn't really seem to care." Tom Mott died in March of 1993 at the age of seventy-one. He got to see his youngest son rise to the top of his profession, win millions of dollars in prize money, and earn the respect and admiration of his peers. That was small consolation to Mott, though. At the age of thirty-nine, he was nowhere near ready to lose the father who made it all possible. Sometimes, even several years later, Mott would catch himself thinking, "What would I trade for just one more day..."

Within a year of Tom Mott's death, both of Tina's parents also passed away.

"I think it really made our marriage strong," Tina said. "We have no one else, so we look to each other all the time for advice. I ask Bill for guidance all the time. He's always right about people."

The Motts hit a bump in the road when, in 1991, bankruptcy proceedings commenced on one of Firestone's companies. By January of 1992, Firestone dispersed sixty of his horses in a sale at Keeneland, while hanging on to such young runners as Paradise Creek, American Chance and Chenin Blanc. He released Mott from the terms of their private arrangement. The cash flow had dried up, stable debts were backed up, and Mott found himself paying bills out of his own pocket and standing in line with other creditors.

"I was owed a lot of money," Mott said. "And I was supporting the horses. I asked Keeneland for some help from the bank. They kind of balked. I made it clear that those horses of Bert's going in their sale might not show up. I got a check pretty soon after that."

The Firestone experience, for all its turmoil, had several happy endings. When word got out that Mott would be public again, the telephone started ringing with offers from potential clients, both new and old. The 1992 season was Mott's best ever, with total purses of $4.8 million. Chenin Blanc stuck around to win almost $700,000. Paradise Creek went on to capture the

Arlington Million and reign as the champion male grass horse of 1994 after being sold by the Firestones to Japanese breeder Masayuki Nishiyama. And were it not for the Firestone opportunity, Mott never would have trained Theatrical.

The son of Nureyev was already proven as a first-rate runner back when Mott took the Firestone job. After a European career, Theatrical raced in California with Bobby Frankel and came within a heartbeat of winning the Breeders' Cup Turf at Santa Anita in November of 1986. Mott got Theatrical in Florida that winter and found him to be a temperamental artist who could change his outlook on life at a moment's notice. Sometimes he behaved. Sometimes he refused to train. At all times he was more than a handful.

Mott backed off and gave Theatrical some space. Soon, it was full-blown psychological warfare. In his first start for Mott, the newly-turned five-year-old was disqualified from second place to fourteenth for interference in the Bougainvillea Handicap at Hialeah Park. After that, he won his next four starts, including the Sword Dancer Handicap at Belmont in which Dance of Life, the actual first-place finisher, was disqualified for interference. There was always something strange going on in a Theatrical race.

Mott experienced one of the worst nightmares of his career in the Budweiser-Arlington Million that summer when Theatrical faced the toughest test of the season. The opposition included Manila, who had beaten Theatrical in the '86 Breeders' Cup. But the real enemy was the newly introduced quarantine barn, where horses were sequestered before each race. Mott braced himself for disaster, and that's what he got.

"Theatrical got in there and completely fell apart," Mott recalled, the pain still evident in his voice. "I mean, the sweat was just pouring off him. At one point he just flat sat down in the stall. I was afraid he would colic, or tie up, or something. When we finally led him over for the race I knew we were in trouble." Theatrical finished third without ever threatening victorious Manila.

Back home, safe and sound in his Belmont Park stall, the moody star knocked off the two biggest grass races of the fall—the Turf Classic and the Man o' War Stakes. He was back on top and ready for the final start of his career, which would be a repeat appearance in the Breeders' Cup Turf. The setting was Hollywood Park.

Allen Paulson had purchased half of Theatrical from Firestone in 1985, but, according to a lease agreement, the horse had been carrying Firestone's silks throughout the 1986 and '87 campaigns. For the Breeders' Cup, Paulson wanted jockey Pat Day wearing his red, white and blue colors. Theatrical was retiring to stud at Brookside Farm. It was time, Paulson said, that the public knew who was calling the shots. Firestone, who owned thirty-five percent at the time, argued that he still had control and that the silks would remain the same. When Mott filled out Theatrical's entry form, Paulson asked the trainer to list his silks. Mott declined, citing an obligation to Firestone, his employer, so Paulson took the issue to the board of stewards. Cue the lawyers.

On the day before the race, attorneys for Firestone and Paulson argued the issue before a special referee appointed by the California Horse Racing Board. Paulson dropped a bomb and offered to buy Firestone out. The attorneys went into contract overdrive. In the meantime, the Breeders' Cup official program was printed with a blank silhouette in the space where Theatrical's colors should have been. There were rumors the horse might even be scratched because of the ownership affair.

Finally, terms were set. Richard Craigo, part of Paulson's legal team, conveyed the agreement to Paulson during the Breeders' Cup Ball at the Beverly Hilton Hotel. It was past midnight before everyone was satisfied. "Color-gate" was over. On the track the following afternoon, Theatrical came through with some drama of his own, beating Trempolino, the hero of the Arc de Triomphe, to end his career in glory. Amidst the distraction of the ownership quarrel, Mott suddenly realized that he had won his first Breeders' Cup race and trained his first champion.

After Theatrical left the racetrack and settled into his life as a stallion at Brookside Farm, Mott made the traditional trainer's request of a breeding right or a share. Paulson's answer: "You'll have to see Bert Firestone about that. Your deal was with him." Mott sighed and decided to let the matter quietly fade away. "I had a feeling Mr. Paulson wouldn't be doing much business with me in the future."

Several months later, as Mott entered the stable gate at Belmont Park, the guard handed him a large, flat package.

Mott pulled up to his barn and neatly unwrapped the plain shipping paper. Inside, beautifully mounted, was a photograph of Theatrical winning the Breeders' Cup Turf. The inscription read: "Best wishes, Allen Paulson."

At first, Mott was stunned. He tried fishing around for a hidden meaning. In the end, he decided it was simply one of those grand cosmic jokes. Anyone who happened to walk by just then would have seen Bill Mott, sitting in the cab of his pick-up truck, all alone and laughing out loud.

CHAPTER 5

AWAKENING

Bill Mott, frustrated jockey, decided one morning that it was time he threw a leg over Cigar to find out just what the big colt could do. It was not unusual. The boss did that a lot. For years he had been a familiar sight at racetracks far and wide, galloping along in his scuffed up helmet and fringed leather leggings, his irons dropped and leading with his jaw. The success of more recent seasons, coupled with the trauma of turning forty, conspired to add a few unwelcome pounds around the middle. But when Mott wanted to know first-hand how a horse was hitting the ground, he never hesitated to mount up.

It was April of 1994. The horses stabled in Florida had shipped north to Belmont Park, where the spring meet would be opening soon. The Belmont main track was still closed to training, so Mott walked Cigar with the other horses in the seven o'clock set down Man o' War Avenue to the one-mile training track. A little while later, Mott returned, his face beaming like a neon sign.

"This is one of the best horses I've been on in a long time," Mott announced as Cigar carried him underneath the shedrow. "He is absolutely automatic. He switches leads at every corner. I mean, he carried me around there effortlessly. I haven't been on a horse like this since Theatrical."

Round and round they went, Cigar calmly cooling down as Mott's praise heated up. Simon Bray, the barn foreman, immediately plugged into Mott's enthusiasm. Tom Albertrani, Mott's number one Belmont assistant, listened to the ravings of the boss and took them with a grain of salt. As Mott would readily confess, he could sometimes talk some serious horseback trash, especially when he stepped back into the role of exercise rider. Anyway, Albertrani, a former jockey, had been galloping Cigar since mid-February. He already knew how smooth the big colt could move. It was still a long way back to the races.

After a routine recovery from his knee surgery, Cigar began jogging at Brookside West in January. At the same time, the Paulsons decided to send more of their horses to New York, where they would be trained by Mott. Madeleine Paulson was a strong advocate of the softer racetracks in the East for the benefit of the horses. She became convinced that Cigar would stand a better chance to fulfill his potential if he trained over more forgiving ground. Mott was her man because of his success with Fraise. And, as of early 1994, Cigar was her horse.

The Paulsons maintained a playfully competitive relationship, whether at golf, cards, tennis or mischievous hints of past relationships. Occasionally Allen would make a gift of a horse to his wife, but more often they contrived a way to make the transaction more interesting. Madeleine, for instance, won Fraise in a golf game in Palm Desert, after which he won more than $2 million in her name. The colors their horses carried were almost identical, with patriotic stars and stripes in red, white and blue. Allen had switched from a "GA" on the front to "AP," while Madeleine's bore her "MP" monogram.

Paulson remained baffled by Cigar's spotty three-year-old form, and he was unsure of the colt's post-operative future. He was inclined to let Madeleine take over Cigar's career, if only to stimulate a possible change of luck. Madeleine called Mott in Florida and told him she had two horses on the way—a filly named Izana and a colt named Cigar. Back in California, Paulson put Cigar out of his mind. More pleasant news was unfolding. In early February, Diazo won the $500,000 Strub Stakes. In early March, Stuka was awarded victory in the $1-million Santa Anita Handicap upon the disqualification of The Wicked North. In the long history of the two races, stretching back nearly fifty years, no owner had ever won both in the same season with two different horses.

Madeleine had her own very special hopes for Cigar. She was not shy about sharing them with Mott.

"She always sets her expectations very high," Mott said. "She said Cigar was good enough to win the Breeders' Cup Mile. Now, sometimes she will just be talking about an unproven horse who is going to do this or that. I can usually tell the difference. In this case, she really believed this horse was a good horse. I'm sure she'd gotten plenty of feedback about Cigar from Alex and the other people around the stable. She knows who to talk to. And everybody in California truly liked this horse."

Especially Alex Hassinger. The thought of losing Cigar, as well as other horses, was a professional blow. With his new knees and added maturity, Cigar clearly was going to be the big horse in the barn for 1994.

"That was disheartening, to be honest," Hassinger said of Cigar's departure. "I thought we did right by the horse and took very good care of him. Any time you make a project out of something you hope to finish it."

Cigar and a group of Paulson horses boarded a cargo plane at Ontario International Airport near Pomona, California, on the afternoon of February 19, 1994, bound for South Florida. Early the next morning, they were bedded down at Hialeah Park in Miami in the care of Mott's assistants, Tom and Fonda Albertrani.

Cigar did not suffer much in the transition. One day he was living in the custom-built beauty of Brookside Farm West. The next day he was strolling among the historic palms and gardens of majestic old Hialeah. Mott had horses at both Hialeah and nearby Gulfstream Park, where the race meeting was revving into high gear. On the day before Cigar arrived, champion Dehere had snapped to life with a victory in the Fountain of Youth Stakes. Holy Bull finished last, but three weeks later he bounced back in a big way to win the Florida Derby.

By the time Cigar came into Mott's life, his far-flung staff had settled into a no-frills efficiency, revolving smoothly around the main stable trained by Mott himself. At first glance, his top help seemed to reflect the personality of the boss, taking their cue from his cool demeanor and consummate hands-on horsemanship. On closer inspection, it became clear that they were simply Bill Mott's kind of people.

The Albertranis had been with Mott the longest without interruption. Tom was a native of Brooklyn who hung up his jockey silks early to learn the training trade. He had worked for Van Berg as a teenager and knew Mott by reputation, but they never did business until Mott sent Heatherten to New York in the spring of 1985 for a series of important stakes. Albertrani galloped the mare while she was there, and she ran well in both of her starts. When Mott moved to New York at the end of 1986 to begin the job with Bert Firestone, Tom Albertrani was front and center applying for a post. Fonda Albertrani joined the team in the summer of 1987.

"Bill had to go back home to New York that August to be with Tina when she had Brady," said Fonda, who came from Hempstead, just down the road from Belmont Park. "I was working for another trainer, and Tommy and Bill had seventeen horses in Saratoga, with just the two of them riding. When Bill left, Tommy said, 'You've got to come to work for me right away!' After that it was just the three of us riding the horses for a year or two before Bill needed to hire any outside help." When the Firestone job disappeared and Mott went back to a public stable, Albertrani was still his right hand man.

Tim Jones had seniority, having joined the Midwest division of Mott's public stable in 1984. A rodeo rider as a teenager, Jones returned home to Arkansas to run a farm for a year, then spent part of a season working for the Midwest stable of D. Wayne Lukas before coming back into the Mott fold. Jones rose to Mott's chief Belmont Park assistant in 1995 when Tom Albertrani took a job with Sheikh Mohammed's Godolphin Stable in Europe and Dubai. During Cigar's championship campaigns, the big horse never traveled anywhere without Tim Jones.

"I got my work ethic from my mother," Jones said. "But I definitely put it to work being with Bill."

Ralph Nicks, who hailed from northeast Texas, caught on with Mott as an exercise rider in 1989. As the Mott stable expanded, Nicks earned a shot as traveling assistant, taking small groups of horses to various Midwestern outposts. Eventually, Nicks and his wife, Judy, would spend most of their year in Kentucky with the Mott horses not suited for competition in New York. Like the Albertranis, both Ralph and Judy brought along talent as exercise riders.

"Bill and me talk every day," Nicks said. "I like to say he gives me just enough rope to hang myself."

Simon Bray was the rookie of the team when Cigar hit the scene. Born just north of London in Hertfordshire, the son of a businessman and horse owner, Bray worked four years for champion English trainer Henry Cecil before casting his sights on American racing. A friend recommended Mott, and Bray headed for Florida in the winter of 1993. He started at the bottom, walking hots and cleaning stalls, and by the spring he was Albertrani's foreman in New York. As far as Bray was concerned, class was in session every day at the world's best university.

"You can't ask for a better mentor than Bill," Bray said. "He's half horse. He can do everything. There's nothing worse than that feeling of being in a job where you're not totally sure of what's going on. Like having a school exam and not having studied enough to learn it. You look up and see all the other guys writing thirty times faster than you. Bill takes that all away. You learn to do things the right way, and not because you're following instructions. You do it because you believe in it. Actually, we call it the Bill Mott Way."

The Mott Way was worth $5.1 million in purses in 1993, sealed by the victory of Fraise in the $500,000 Hollywood Turf Cup in December. The total was good enough for fifth-place in the national standings behind Robert Frankel, Richard Mandella, Shug McGaughey and Ron McAnally. Mott's ever-growing organization was running smoothly, with more than forty owners and well over a hundred horses in various stages of training at four different locations. Mott ran the main string of about forty horses at Gulfstream with the help of Ralph and Judy Nicks. The Albertranis cared for twenty horses at Hialeah. At Payson Park training center, Tim Jones and former jockey Dave Wallace wintered with a large group, while Simon Bray kept the home fires burning back at Belmont Park in chilly New York. After closing up shop in Florida, the Albertranis would move to Belmont Park, Jones and Wallace would train the New York overflow at Saratoga, and the Nickses would head for the Midwest.

Upon their return to Belmont in April of '94, Mott and the Albertranis began to peel back the intrigue presented by

Cigar. They had gone through the identical process with literally hundreds of horses, whether it was a mature, proven commodity such as Theatrical or a youth project such as Paradise Creek. Mott could read the past performances. He knew Cigar was capable of running in stakes company on the grass. He was a striking physical specimen who moved with fluid grace. Around the barn, he behaved with good sense and class.

"You could have dragged a guy off the street to walk him," Bray said. "He just went through the motions."

Cigar battled a minor virus that spring. He was diagnosed with an ulcer—a relatively common affliction among thoroughbred racehorses—and put on a medication regimen that seemed to quell the problem. The rest of the inventory was straightforward. He had the cryotherapy marks on his left hock, the jagged scar on the right side of the chest, and flat, dry growth on the left side of his neck that later was biopsied and found to be harmlessly benign. The only recent medical history of note had to do with his knees. And when it came to Cigar's knees, Mott was amazed.

"Whatever he had cleaned up very well," Mott said. "Literally, if you looked at his knees you could not tell a thing. In fact, I often wondered if he'd even had surgery at all."

Fonda Albertrani's first impression of Cigar was her delight over his distinctive name. Later, as they became a familiar couple each morning during exercise hours, he became the highlight of her day.

"I thought he was fun to ride," she said. "He always gave the impression that he was going to be a tough horse to handle.

But he never was. He would grab the bit and you'd think, 'Oh, boy. This horse is gonna fly.' Then as soon as he realized what he was supposed to do, he would relax. The mistake some riders would make would be to let him have his way. Then he'd take off and you'd never get him back. But if he knew you had him, he was always under control. I don't think it was intentional, either. He'd go up the track real slow. Then all of a sudden he'd seize the bit. You had to be prepared and sit tight. Then, after about an eighth of a mile, he'd relax, throw the bit away, and just go along like a baby.

"He was a challenge," Fonda added, "but a neat challenge. Some horses are dead-brained and dead-mouthed. They're gonna do their thing no matter what you want to do, and all you feel like is a passenger. I never felt like a passenger on Cigar. There was always some sort of sensitivity, a relationship, between horse and rider."

When Fonda finished with Cigar's daily gallops, Simon Bray would take over and hold his head while his groom, Juan Campuzano, gave the big colt a bath. It did not take Bray long to realize Cigar was blessed with a special personality.

"People say horses are intelligent," Bray began. "But really, they're dumb half the time. They are creatures of routine, and if you keep them in a good routine they look smart. Believe me, though, when I say that Cigar is very, very smart. Nothing fazes him. You could throw a three-year-old kid in the stall and leave him there. Cigar wouldn't touch him. Bill, myself or Tim can come along and he might try and bite. In that way he's extremely clever. He knows what he can get away with and what he can't. He'll stand on the track as loose horses go flying by and he won't move a muscle. When it comes time to get ready to race he knows it well in advance. He understands not only that there's been a change in the routine, but what the change actually means. And it was amazing how his attitude changed when he started winning."

Unfortunately, that did not occur until after he lost four more races, each one "less than mediocre," as far as Fonda Albertrani was concerned. Mott ran Cigar for the first time on July 8, 1994, in a mile and one-sixteenth turf race at Belmont Park. Cigar was favored, he showed speed, and he stopped like he was dead tired, beating one horse in the process. On August 8 at Saratoga, Cigar tried a similar group at a mile and one-eighth and finished third, beaten three lengths. Mott thought maybe, with a little better racing luck, he might have won. But just maybe.

Back at Belmont Park, Cigar was entered in a one-mile turf race on September 16. If he was going to fulfill Madeleine Paulson's dream of competing in the Breeders' Cup Mile, now was the time for him to shine. Instead, Cigar piddled away another opportunity and finished seventh in a field of eleven. Jerry Bailey, who rode him for the first time, was not impressed. Mott was left talking to himself.

"I'm thinking, 'What's going on?' For a grass horse he seemed much too anxious. He was always up on the bridle, running off, and then flattening out. It didn't make sense. He was training too good and feeling too good to be running so bad. He was becoming a real topic of conversation with my assistants."

There is no proof—no notarized statements or sworn documents—that recorded exactly who first suggested running Cigar on the dirt. "Fonda distinctly recalls asking me why we didn't try him on the dirt," Mott said with a laugh. "I don't think that was the first time it was mentioned." Certainly, the subject was broached back in California. Madeleine Paulson may have tossed out the possibility during that frustrating summer of '94. Among the people in the Mott stable, credit for the idea seemed to flit back and forth. In the satisfying wake of Cigar's transformation, the answer really did not matter.

Neither is it surprising that it took Mott so long to make the decision. "Sometimes Bill needed that last little push from someone to try something new," Fonda recalled. About the only thing Mott did quickly was drive his high-powered Lincoln with the pedal to the floor and his mind miles away. The question of Cigar's best surface was a nagging, knotty lump in his craw. The alternatives were fitting Cigar in blinkers, or perhaps running him in a high-priced claiming race to restore his self esteem with an easy win over inferior competition. On October 7, Mott gave Julie Krone a chance to find the key at a mile and a sixteenth on the Belmont grass. Same old story. Cigar pressed the pace and slowed to a crawl, splitting the field of six. Fonda was adamant. "Try the dirt!" Mott was running out of options. Cigar certainly was not a horse who deserved to compete in the Breeders' Cup Mile. At that point, he was just barely better than an empty stall. His good looks and gentlemanly demeanor had taken him as far as they could.

Three thousand miles away in Bonsall, Alex Hassinger was tending to some late-morning bookwork in the accounting office of Brookside Farm West. Since Cigar's departure the California stable had enjoyed modest success, but nothing spectacular. Hassinger and the Paulsons were excited about the emergence of Miss Dominique, who was named for Madeleine's daughter. Hassinger was making plans to take the five-year-old mare to Churchill Downs, where she would face the best of her division in the Breeders' Cup Distaff on November 5. He was on his way out when the telephone rang. A co-worker answered and called out, "It's for you."

"Who is it?"

"Bill Mott."

The call was brief. Mott wanted Hassinger's honest assessment of Cigar's maiden race win on the Hollywood Park main track on that May afternoon nearly a year and a half before. Hassinger told Mott it was a good race and the horse handled the dirt well. Thank you. Good luck. Good-bye.

It was time. There were just six horses running in the sixth race at Aqueduct on the clear, comfortable afternoon of October 28, Fonda Albertrani's birthday. The race was at one mile...on the dirt. Cigar was vanned over from his Belmont stall earlier in the day, and by race time the Mott crew had gathered in the box seats. Around them, making little dent in the towering grandstand, a crowd of 6,832 joined with their off-track brethren to make Cigar their 7-to-2 second choice. Mike Smith, who had ridden Cigar in a pair of worthless turf tries, was back on board. Cigar left the gate like a Titan rocket and did not stop until he had won the race by eight lengths. The Mott crowd could hardly believe their eyes.

"I was so relieved he had finally *done* something," Fonda recalled.

"He won by how many?!" exclaimed Madeleine Paulson when she got the news.

"Now what do we do with him?" wondered Mott, who packed up the next day and headed for Churchill Downs to run Paradise Creek and Fraise in the Breeders' Cup Turf.

A change in surface has done wonders for many great horses in the past. John Henry was a mediocre dirt horse until he began winning championships on the grass. The stretch-running gray horse Vigors was a stakes winner on the turf at a younger age, but he turned into a superstar when switched to the main track. Criminal Type came to America from European grass racing with nothing to brag about. On American dirt he became Horse of the Year.

Theories for such turnarounds abound. Some experts insist the size and shape of the equine foot dictates the ground over which they will excel. The flatter and wider the hoof, the more the horse will prefer the turf. Runners with high, lifting knee action may do better on long grass than those who merely glide along, barely elevating their feet. Still others simply need time to mature. Neither surface nor distance makes a particular difference until the animal has been allowed to age, like a respectable wine. Ack Ack was basically a sprinter at ages three and four, then turned into a mile and a quarter monster at age five when he was the 1971 Horse of the Year.

Cigar may have combined elements from all of the above. His stride was long and low, and his foot was far from flat. Without question, he needed time and careful handling to be at peace with his growing pains. Still, Cigar's allowance race win, though impressive, was no reason to think the transformation was suddenly complete. As a racing moment, it receded immediately into the background with the running of the Breeders' Cup eight days later, on November 5. Down in Kentucky, Paradise Creek finished third, Fraise ran eleventh, and Miss Dominique jumped up to finish third in the Distaff for Hassinger and the Paulsons at odds of 77-to-1.

Shortly after the event, both Paradise Creek and Fraise were shipped off to prepare for the Japan Cup in Tokyo on November 27. Before leaving for the Orient, Tom Albertrani lobbied hard to run Cigar in the $250,000 NYRA Mile, scheduled for November 26 at Aqueduct. Everyone called it the "Nigh-ruh" Mile in deference to the unwieldy formality of the "New York Racing Association."

Mott balked. As far as he was concerned, Cigar had beaten a weak allowance field late in the year, when competition was notoriously thin. The NYRA Mile was a Grade I event and the last rich prize of the New York season, offering one last swing at some serious shipping money before many of the stables packed off to Florida for the winter. As such, the Mile traditionally drew a large field of thoroughly experienced sprinters and middle-distance specialists. Mott had plenty of advice. His friends among the ranks of handicappers and high-rollers raved over Cigar's October 28 dirt performance. On paper, they said, he was up to the challenge. He would also be a price.

"I guess whatever we might have won on him in the allowance race on the dirt didn't exactly make up for what we'd lost on him in his four grass races," Mott said with a sheepish grin.

As Thanksgiving approached, the Albertranis headed for Tokyo with the Japan Cup runners. Mott followed a few days later, leaving Simon Bray behind to do the honors for the NYRA Mile. Cigar responded with a seven-length victory over favored Devil His Due and ten others. His odds were nearly 9-to-1.

As soon as Cigar cooled down, Bray started to spread the good news around the globe. He reached Mott in Tokyo, where Japan Cup day was just getting under way, and Mott passed the word to Tom and Fonda. Out in California, relaxing in their Palm Springs condo, the Paulsons were having a quiet weekend, awaiting the news about Fraise's race in Japan. Somehow, Madeleine got her dates crossed and thought the NYRA Mile was supposed to be run November 27 as well. While Allen and his poodles, Frosty and Lucky, lounged on the living room couch, Madeleine put in a late afternoon call to the Mott barn. Bray answered.

"Simon, when does Cigar run tomorrow?" she asked.

"He won!" Bray shrieked, abandoning all British decorum.

Madeleine thought him terribly confused.

"No, no. I mean what time tomorrow does he run?"

"He won!" Bray insisted. "He won by seven!"

Madeleine started screaming for joy.

"Cigar won the NYRA Mile! My horse won the NYRA Mile!"

The poodles stirred. Allen Paulson forced a smile. As the breeder of Cigar, he was a proud and happy man. As the former owner, he was wondering what on Earth had possessed him to give away a Grade I winner, even to his wife. Soon a new deal was struck. Allen would trade his champion filly and young broodmare, Eliza, straight up for Cigar. He threw in a breeding to Theatrical, just to sweeten the offer. Madeleine accepted the terms, and the next time Jerry Bailey showed up to ride Cigar, the "MP" on his chest had become "AP" again.

CHAPTER 6

CONTROL

It began as just another ordinary post parade on a quiet spring day at Keeneland Racecourse in Lexington. Jerry Bailey was perched atop a two-year-old colt, his right stirrup slightly higher than his left in the classic acey-deucy style, his hands calm at the reins as they were led onto the track.

The colt was Gregory Hines, named for the dancer turned actor and all-around entertainer. Gregory Hines, the horse, had a long way to go to live up to his name. He was about to make the first start of his life, and even though it was an insignificant race in the broad scheme of the sport, it was serious business for Bailey. He knew too well that anything could happen on horseback. As a veteran of twenty-one years, he had witnessed some gruesome racing accidents. As president of the Jockeys' Guild, he was faced on a daily basis with the cries of help from injured and disabled riders. And, as a thirty-seven-year-old husband and father of a miracle son just two and a half years old, he was not inclined to risk it all by letting his mind wander.

Gregory Hines seemed cool enough as he joined the five-horse post parade. Bailey had no reason to be suspicious. Then something began to stir, and Gregory Hines started to dance. Bailey applied some pressure to the reins in an attempt to assert control. Suddenly, the colt dipped to the left, leaving Bailey aloft, hanging in mid-air. Reacting as he had dozens of times before, Bailey tried to save both himself and the horse from serious damage. As he spilled toward the ground he clung to the reins. The idea was to keep Gregory Hines from running off alone and risking real catastrophe. It was the wrong move.

Had Bailey let go he would have fallen clear. Instead, he ended up bouncing along the side of Gregory Hines in treacherous proximity to the terrified animal. When Bailey finally lost his grip on the reins he was still in the danger zone. Gregory Hines swerved again and lashed out with his back legs. He caught Bailey flush in the chest with both hind feet. Henry Aaron, swinging for the fences, could not have made better contact. The whole thing happened in less than two blinks.

Bailey laid in the mud, stunned, trying to catch his breath. When a jockey goes down—and stays conscious—he immediately takes inventory. Can I move my legs? Can I move my hands? My neck? Is there an inordinate amount of blood flowing from unseen wounds? Are there any bones sticking out? Do I remember my name?

On this particular day, on this particular occasion, one more thing entered Bailey's mind and quickly shoved everything else aside. His first thought when he tumbled into the soupy Keeneland mud went off like a siren wailing in his head:

Will I be able to ride Cigar on Saturday?

The date was April 12, 1995, three days shy of Cigar's scheduled start in the $750,000 Oaklawn Handicap at Oaklawn Park in Hot Springs, Arkansas, located about six hundred miles south of Keeneland. Cigar had been training at Oaklawn for two weeks and working well. Bill Mott was already on the scene. Allen Paulson was heading into town and would be joined for the race by his pal, former Chrysler Corporation chairman Lee Iacocca. All they needed was the jock.

Covered with mud, Bailey was scooped up by the track ambulance and taken to the Keeneland first aid station. The blow from the hooves, shod with sharp mud calks, sliced a hole in Bailey's protective flak vest. He was transferred to another ambulance and taken to a local hospital for X-rays.

"Believe me, I thought I'd broken my sternum." Bailey remembers the pain vividly. He was skeptical when X-rays showed no fractures. He went home, but he could hardly breathe. Suzee, his wife, took him back to the hospital. The answer was the same: no fractures. Go home and rest.

Bailey spent an agonizing night with his chest packed in ice and wrapped with an Ace bandage. The next day he stayed home in their Lexington season rental. He called Mott.

"I won't ride the big horse unless I feel I can do him justice."

"I'll get somebody just in case," Mott replied.

"I'll take today off," Bailey went on. "Then if I feel better I'll try riding tomorrow."

"Fine," Mott said. "You can let me know tomorrow."

So, while Mott made plans for an emergency replacement, Bailey laid low that Thursday, keeping his chest iced and popping nothing more than the occasional Advil. By Friday morning the pain was not so bad. On Friday afternoon, Bailey tried riding at Keeneland. On Friday night he called Mott again:

"I'll be there."

Suzee Bailey had seen it all before. A jockey and his family live with the constant threat of physical trauma. "He goes to bed with ice all the time," Suzee once said, laughing at how it sounded. A former actress, she was doing SportsChannel television when they met in Florida in 1984. He was winning the Flamingo Stakes on Time for a Change. Later on, they enjoyed the irony of the name.

They were married on December 17, 1985, two days after a cast was removed from the groom's left foot. Her only complaint: "It was a little tough to dance." At five-foot-six, a hundred and nine pounds, Bailey had a tolerance for pain that rivaled the stoicism of the Russians during the German siege of St. Petersburg. The medicine cabinet of his comfortable home in suburban Long Island was crammed full of unopened bottles of prescription painkillers, offered in good faith by sympathetic doctors. Bailey just said no thanks. "He's just like Cigar," Suzee observed, dead serious. "He keeps going." Ice, rest, rehab and the occasional dose of over-the-counter ibuprofen was Bailey's recipe when the inevitable accidents occurred. And they have happened with regularity, although not catastrophically, throughout a career that began in 1974 at Sunland Park in New Mexico, just across the state line from his childhood home in El Paso, Texas. For instance:

In 1976, when he was riding first call for the powerful Florida stable of Arnold Winick, Bailey fractured his jaw in a

morning workout at Hialeah when a horse stepped squarely on his face. At the time he had won the featured stakes
race on four successive weekends. End of momentum.

In 1984, firmly established in New York, Bailey was
ready to take the Saratoga meet by storm. The dream died
when his very first mount on opening day, Will of Iron, went
to his knees at the break and shot Bailey to the ground like
a javelin. Will of Iron got up and kept going. Bailey broke
his collarbone and five ribs.

In 1985, Bailey was involved in the horrendous wreck of
the Fall Highweight Handicap at Belmont Park. He was riding Charging Falls, and they were in the thick of the race
when a horse named First Guess broke a leg right in front of
them. Charging Falls somersaulted over the fallen horse and
ejected Bailey into the path of another runner, Pancho Villa.
Pancho Villa stepped on Bailey, breaking three ribs and three
vertebrae. Bailey also broke three bones in his left foot.

The piratical scar on his forehead is from a tumble in
1986, when a horse broke down beneath him on the
Belmont Park grass course and another horse struck him
between the eyes. But the small lines on either side of his
strong German nose are of slightly more benign origin.
Blame them on his dog, a spoiled cocker spaniel named
Barney, who took Bailey's playful growls too seriously one
evening and attacked the first thing he saw. Doghouse for
Barney. Seventeen stitches for Bailey.

Jerry Dale Bailey was born on August 29, 1957, in Dallas,
Texas. His father, a dentist, owned quarter horses, but

young Jerry was more interested in baseball, basketball and track. His first steady source of income came from betting the Green Bay Packers of the mid-1960s while his school chums slavishly backed the Cowboys. "Bart Starr and Donnie Anderson against those guys? Come on." He gloats to this day and wears green and gold around the house.

He was tall for his family but small compared to the rest of the world, especially when it came to prep athletics. He wrestled in high school because the playing field was level. But what he really wanted was a crack at big-time team sports. What he got was a push toward the racetrack.

The involvement of Dr. James Bailey in quarter horses gave his teenage son a foot in the door. Jerry was riding match races on quarter horses by the time he was twelve. There was nothing to it, he says, "Just sit and hit for four hundred yards." Bailey had a natural grace and youthful resilience that stood out around the weather-beaten veterans of the Texas-New Mexico circuit. So did his long, 1970s style hair and soft, almost androgynously handsome features. The kid had matinee idol written all over him.

But first he needed to learn the ropes. Matching quarter horses could get him only so far. The world of thoroughbreds called, and Bailey was listening. He began paying close attention to Ray York, a no-nonsense warrior who was well on his way to winning more than three thousand races in a career that began in 1947. York, a regular in California and points East, ended up in New Mexico in the early 1970s after doing stunt work for a John Wayne movie called "The Cowboys." He hooked up with a live stable and stuck around to ride.

"I lived in El Paso back then," York recalled. "It turned out Jerry and my youngest boy went to the same high school, a year apart. He was one of a lot of kids who wanted to ride. Good-looking kid, too. But we never rode against each other.

"Jerry always had the talent, but he also had the brains. That's something I didn't have. When I was a kid I watched Johnny Longden, Eddie Arcaro, Bill Shoemaker, and Jack Westrope. Jerry's style is along the lines of Arcaro, or Bill Boland. And I'll throw a little bit of Jack Westrope in there because Jerry can really switch a stick, from left to right or right to left. Those guys were in constant, forward movement with the horse. And Jerry's style is quite a bit like that."

Still, it was a big jump going from a Ray York wannabe to wearing silks in the afternoon. Chuck Sherman, a local jock's agent, saw enough in Bailey's morning exercise work to take him under his wing. Sherman called in some favors and hustled a few mounts. Bailey held up his end of the deal by winning his first official thoroughbred race in his first try on a horse named Fetch at Sunland Park, and then winning with his second mount as well. It was November of 1974.

Bailey's early travels took him to Ak-Sar-Ben in Omaha, Nebraska, where he was the leading apprentice jockey of 1975. Bill Mott was there at the same time, galloping horses for Jack Van Berg and training a couple of his own on the side. Mott remembered John Lively, David Whited, even Mary Bacon in the local riding pool. But he did not remember much about Bailey until they got to talking one day about the great Omaha tornado of '75.

"Of course, if you're in the Midwest long enough you're going to have a twister in common with almost anybody," Mott said. "The day this one hit, Jerry was in the tunnel leading to the jocks' room and I was in the tunnel at the three-eighths pole leading to the infield. From down where I was it felt like the racetrack was going to blow away."

Having weathered a summer of Midwestern storms, Bailey headed for hurricane country in the winter of 1976 and connected with the Florida stable of trainer Arnold Winick. The Winick horses took Bailey on a successful ride to California, Chicago and back to Florida again. His next step was to New Jersey, the threshold of big-time New York racing. He admired such giants as Angel Cordero, Eddie Maple and Jorge Velasquez from across the Hudson River. Occasionally, they would come to New Jersey and win the big races, while the local riders sat on the sidelines and watched.

Bailey made the leap to New York in the spring of 1982. He was good enough to penetrate the top ten standings, although the choice mounts usually went to the other guys. The key was getting to know MacKenzie Miller, who trained the Rokeby Stable horses of Paul Mellon, the renowned philanthropist and patron of the arts, owner and breeder of such grand thoroughbreds as Mill Reef, Arts and Letters and Fort Marcy. Whether he knew it or not, Bailey was about to start playing in a whole different league.

"I think Jerry was ready," said Miller, a Hall of Fame trainer who retired in 1995, a few months after introducing Bailey as the Hall of Fame's newest member. "He was quiet, intelligent, just cocky enough, and horses ran for him. I used him without hesitation."

Used him well, too. First there was Fit to Fight, winner of the Metropolitan, Suburban and Brooklyn Handicaps in 1984. Then there was Hero's Honor, a very fast grass horse, and Glowing Tribute, a top mare, and Danger's Hour, another accomplished horse on grass. The best of Bailey's Rokeby horses was Eastern Echo, a precocious two-year-old of 1990 who fractured his ankle before he could make it to the Kentucky Derby. Bailey and Miller became a constant team. At the end of each morning, when the horses were put up and fed, the jockey would stop by the Rokeby stable cottage at Belmont Park to have a quiet chat with the boss. They'd talk about anything and everything. And sometimes they would talk about the Kentucky Derby.

On a table in a corner of Bailey's office at home in Muttontown, New York, a bronze sculpture of a horse in full flight is displayed. Every time Bailey looks up from his desk, his eyes fall squarely on the sculpture. If he could, he would wear it around his neck, or carry it in his pocket. It means that much to him.

The horse is Sea Hero, who gave Bailey, Miller and Mellon their first Kentucky Derby win in 1993. The sculpture was a gift from Paul Mellon, delivered by Miller to Bailey one afternoon at Belmont Park in a large, elegant carrying bag. On the wooden base of the sculpture was etched a personal message from Mellon, thanking Bailey for making "an old owner" so happy. Mellon was eighty-five and nearing the end of his life as a horse owner when Sea Hero and Bailey galloped to victory on that bright May afternoon.

Mellon's gratitude seemed to know no end. He sent a driver to the Baileys' home just to drop off a set of six sterling silver julep cups, with a "thank you" engraved from Sea Hero. Later in the year, Mellon invited the Baileys to his Virginia estate and gave them a personal tour of his private art museum. Suzee was nervous when little Justin Bailey, still a toddler, strayed too close to the Degas and tried touching the Rodin. Mellon laughed and said let him play. It was never too early to expose children to fine art.

"This business is remarkable, the places it can take you." Bailey was musing about the range of personalities he would encounter on a typical racing day. "I can be talking that morning to a groom in a stall with a third grade education who knows as much about horses as anyone. That afternoon, I'll be with Mr. Mellon, or Joe Allbritton, or Allen Paulson."

Paulson, for obvious reasons, became a dedicated Bailey fan. As a test pilot who had to make quick decisions under pressure, Paulson saw some of the same traits in his jockey. "He's always so cool, and he's always in the right place, isn't he?" Paulson said after one of Cigar's wins. "He never gets in trouble."

Bailey is very cool. Maybe too cool, sometimes. Raised in a strict, quiet household, he was conditioned from a young age to keep his emotions tightly bottled. When he started winning big-money races, he would dismiss the moment almost immediately. He couldn't wait to leave the track and wrap himself in his own circle of friends and private life.

The Baileys still considered themselves newlyweds in the summer of 1986 when they spent their first Saratoga season together. He responded by riding Wise Times to victory in the Travers Stakes, the biggest race of the meeting. Suzee fought her way through the crowd and down on the rail to greet her husband after he dismounted and weighed in. She reached up to kiss his mud-splattered face, and as she did, Jerry said, "You'd better leave now before the traffic hits."

It was typical Bailey, refusing to take time to savor the moment. Clearly, the home-grown emotional reticence of his youth was heightened by the pressures of the racetrack, where glory was both fleeting and infrequent. The day after winning a big race, Bailey always expected to be loudly booed by the crowd the moment he lost on a favorite. Choice mounts disappeared on the whim of an owner or a trainer for a perceived slight or a bitter loss.

It was hard to take for Suzee Bailey. Coming from a demonstrative family scene, brewed from a mix of Italian and Central European blood, she was frustrated that Jerry could never let down and enjoy the good times for all they were worth.

"You're sure low when you're not doing well," she would tell her husband. "Why not appreciate it more when something good happens?"

Bailey tried hard to answer the question.

"I'm a classic example of a person who would beat himself up far more for a loss than I would enjoy myself after a win. How I got that way? I don't know. Nothing ever came real easily for me. My dad was tough on me, but he was tough on himself. He was a boxer. He worked his way through college, after his father told him flat out not to go, and then wouldn't go to his son's graduation."

Bailey's mother died in 1975 of breast cancer, at age forty-one, when her son was just starting to ride professionally. Her mother, Bailey's grandmother, reached her nineties living alone on a fifteen hundred acre farm in Texas and watching her grandson whenever NBC, ABC or CBS televised a race. No cable in her neighborhood. It was a close count, but Bailey got the feeling that Hulda Seawright—his "Gramcracker"— was always one of his biggest fans.

As a young rider, Bailey had a reputation for being aloof. He maintained a careful distance from the people with whom he worked.

"People thought he was arrogant," said Gary Young, a private clocker, gambler and bloodstock advisor who met Bailey when he rode for the Winick stable in Chicago. "They saw him as the 'chosen one' riding for the big outfit. A baby-faced, good-looking young guy. And because he didn't feel like palling around with everyone at the racetrack, everyone immediately assumed that as a sign of being stuck up. But let's face it. He's a lot more intelligent than your average rider."

Bailey was smart enough to recognize in 1989 that he needed to make a drastic change in his lifestyle. He described himself back then as a party animal, but he knows there is always more to the problem of alcohol than simply a burning desire to have a real good time. His career seemed stalled on "journeyman," that dreaded designation for workaday jockeys who made a good living but watched the superstars from the outside. He had yet to ride the winner of a Breeders' Cup race or a Triple Crown event. He sustained injuries that killed the momentum of three successive seasons. And at home, he and Suzee were desperately trying to start a family through all sorts of fertility programs.

With the help of Suzee, his closest friends, and an out-patient rehabilitation program, Bailey stopped drinking. If it was hard, he does not dwell on the agony. He is convinced, though, that it was necessary to quit to save his career and himself. Of course, as he admitted later, he was the last one to figure it out.

On a visit to the farm owned by veteran jockey Vince Bracciale, Bailey was invited to taste some of his host's homemade vintage.

"No thanks, Jimbo. I quit drinking last year."

Bracciale paused in mid-pour and looked at his younger friend.

"You know, if there was anyone who should have quit drinking, it was you."

The question of fertility lingered. Eventually, the Baileys considered adoption. Then, in the winter of 1992, while Bailey was riding at the Gulfstream meet in Florida, they tried a new procedure. A few weeks later, Justin Bailey was conceived. He was born November 28, 1992.

The Bailey home sits on three acres of wooded land tucked away off the main road to Oyster Bay on the North

Shore of Long Island. The large yard and patio was customized for the private pleasure of one young boy and two active dogs. The tri-level house is wrapped warmly in dark, weathered wood and decorated in sort of a Martha Stewart-meets-F.A.O. Schwartz atmosphere. Downstairs there is a lounge and office where adults seem relatively safe. Here and there are souvenirs from Bailey's association with Cigar, including the gold-plated riding whip designed by Garrard's that was presented to the winning jockey after the Dubai World Cup.

Bailey worked hard to maintain a sense of suburban normalcy for his family in the face of his dangerous profession. Neighbors knew who he was—especially in the era of Cigar—but he preferred public anonymity whenever possible.

The Baileys were comfortable long before Cigar came along. Between the beginning of 1990 and the end of 1994 his mounts had earned $55,422,833. A jockey's cut of that runs around eight percent. Bailey had prospered because of his work aboard horses like Hansel, winner of the 1991 Preakness and Belmont Stakes; Sultry Song, who earned most of his $1.6-million under Bailey; Home At Last, hero of the $1-million Super Derby in 1990; and such fast, well-bred fillies as Meadow Star, Dispute and Educated Risk. Between 1991 and 1994, Bailey won three editions of the $3-million Breeders' Cup Classic, collecting nearly a half-million dollars from that prestigious event alone.

As a result, Bailey lived as well as he wanted to, had his clothes custom tailored, and though he never ate much, he

Barbara D. Livingston

One streak ends as another begins—an Aqueduct victory on October 28, 1994, follows eight straight losses

Bob/Adam Coglianese

Dueling with Holy Bull early in the Donn Handicap

Barbara D. Livingston

In the paddock before the NYRA Mile

Barbara D. Livingston

Gulfstream Park—first stroke of a perfect season in '95

Barbara D. Livingston

Parading to post for the Gulfstream Park Handicap

Leslie Martin

Packing the house at Suffolk for the Massachusetts Handicap

Barbara D. Livingston

Overpowering a tough field in the Oaklawn Handicap

Barbara D. Livingston

Posing after the Pimlico Special

Barbara D. Livingston

Streaking to the west—Cigar wins the Hollywood Gold Cup

Stidham & Associates

Dominating the field in the Breeders' Cup Classic

Trent Hermann

Making it 10 in a row in the Woodward at Belmont

Trent Hermann

Adding the Jockey Club Gold Cup

Skip Dickstein

**Returning with style
in the '96 Donn**

Barbara D. Livingston

**Making history in the
Arlington Citation
Challenge**

Anne M. Eberhardt

**Exulting in the international
glory of the Dubai World Cup**

Trevor Jones

A triumphant hero returns to Boston

Patricia McQueen

Palace Music, the sire of Cigar

Tony Leonard

A 10-day-old Cigar, with his dam, Solar Slew, in Maryland

Ellen Blackwell Pons

Foaling barn at Country Life Farm, and Richard Harris, the man who was there when Cigar was born

Ellen Blackwell Pons (above) Jay Hovdey

**Brookside Farm
in Kentucky**

Brant Gamma

**Mac (left) and Ted Carr gave
Cigar his early lessons**

Anne M. Eberhardt

Allen Paulson (2nd from left), with his mother, Lillian, and three brothers

Photos courtesy of Allen Paulson

Harry Paulson, Allen's father

Serving his country in the Army Air Corps

Flying high in 1982 in a Gulfstream Peregrine

Taking off with his prized poodles, Lucky and Frosty

In the cockpit of a Gulfstream IV

With his crew after a world-record trip around the globe that included a refueling stop in Dubai

Enjoying the '92 Breeders' Cup at Gulfstream Park with Madeleine

Anne M. Eberhardt

Arazi, carrying the Paulson silks to victory in the '91 Breeders' Cup Juvenile

Anne M. Eberhardt

Bonding with Cigar

Patricia McQueen

**Cigar, looking sharp
in his first career
win on May 9, 1993**

Stidham & Associates

**Alex Hassinger, guiding
Cigar early with a
patient hand**

Barbara D. Livingston

**Close, but no Cigar—
the future champ at
Santa Anita before a
second-place finish
in the '93 Volante on
Breeders' Cup weekend**

Patricia McQueen

The late Thomas and Olive Mott, with sons Bill, Don and Rob (right), and grandson Patrick, in a mid-'80s reunion

Photos Courtesy of the Mott Family

Bill and Tina Mott, with sons Riley (left) and Brady

Bill, at 15, stands proud with his first winner, My Assets; (upper left) a 3-year-old Bill poses with Gretchen, the family dog

Ray Goehring, Bill's boss in the '60s—"All we ever did was talk horses"

Barbara D. Livingston

Working with Jack Van Berg gave Bill a taste of the big time

Barbara D. Livingston

The hands-on horseman, with his first pony, Ol' Red, and today

Barbara D. Livingston

A Saratoga morning
for Cigar and exercise
rider Dave Wallace

Barbara D. Livingston

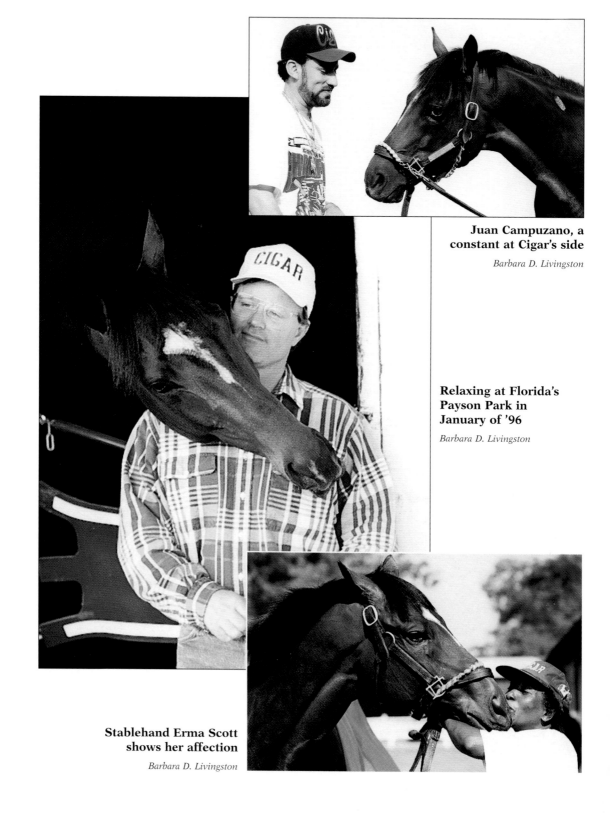

**Juan Campuzano, a
constant at Cigar's side**

Barbara D. Livingston

**Relaxing at Florida's
Payson Park in
January of '96**

Barbara D. Livingston

**Stablehand Erma Scott
shows her affection**

Barbara D. Livingston

An early-morning bath at Belmont Park

Barbara D. Livingston

Getting focused for the work ahead, under Gerard Guenther

Barbara D. Livingston

Showing his power, with Judy Nicks in the saddle

Barbara D. Livingston

Jerry Bailey, dressed for success, with parents James and Betty, and sisters Becky and Kathy

Riders up—3-year-old Jerry on his first horse, a Shetland pony named Lady

Photos Courtesy of the Bailey Family

"Does he know me? Of course he knows me," Jerry says of Cigar

Skip Dickstein

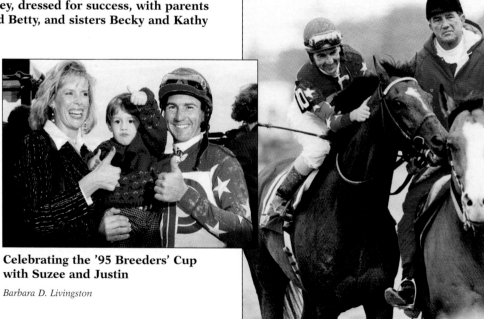

Celebrating the '95 Breeders' Cup with Suzee and Justin

Barbara D. Livingston

Induction into racing's Hall of Fame

Skip Dickstein

With trainer MacKenzie Miller, after Sea Hero's Kentucky Derby win in '93

Anne M. Eberhardt

An ever-present danger—caught flush by Gregory Hines at Keeneland

AP by Matt Barton

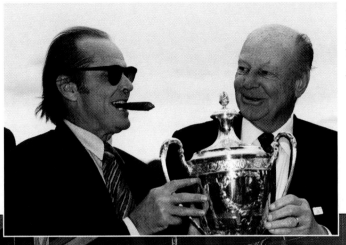

Cigar-mania—Allen Paulson and actor Jack Nicholson after the Woodward

Barbara D. Livingston

Getting a hero's welcome at Gulfstream Park

Equi-Photo

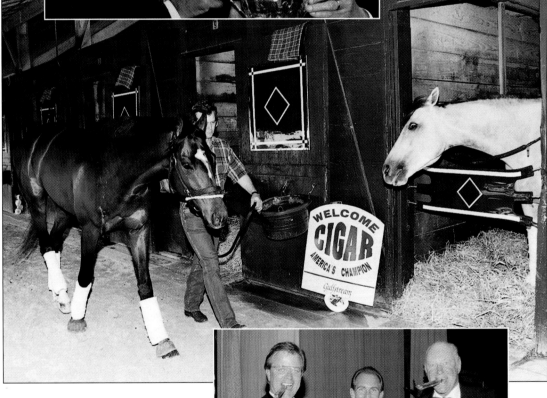

WELCOME
CIGAR
AMERICA'S CHAMPION

Gulfstream

Three cheers—plenty of statues and stogies at the Eclipse Awards

Benoit & Associates

The Dubai World Cup, a "dream result" for Sheikh Mohammed and the Cigar entourage

Trevor Jones

Casting a giant shadow in the Arabian desert

Trevor Jones

Chicago fans giving Cigar a 20-minute ovation after his 16th straight win

Anne M. Eberhardt

Working out before a crowd of several thousand one morning at Saratoga

Barbara D. Livingston

Classic upset—losing to Dare And Go at Del Mar

Anne M. Eberhardt

Eating the key to the city on Cigar Day at Saratoga

Barbara D. Livingston

In the spotlight, with Mott stable assistant Tim Jones

Barbara D. Livingston

could afford the best. He maintained a buttoned-down demeanor, speaking loudest when he addressed issues of jockey safety and welfare for the Jockeys' Guild. He became president of the organization in 1989, upon the retirement of Bill Shoemaker.

Bailey's personality fit well with his riding style. He learned to ride smart, preferring small, unobtrusive moves to secure good position early in a race rather than more desperate, last-second measures. When changing the position of his hands as the race advances, he does not throw his reins in the operatic manner of Kent Desormeaux or Chris Antley. He takes the occasional peek under his arm to gauge the progress and position of the competition, but never more than once or twice a race, while fellow Hall of Famer Chris McCarron keeps almost constant watch.

Bailey stands tall for a jockey and therefore he must stay very slim. It takes constant attention to the health of his lower back and his legs to fold his frame level with the back of the horse, reducing as much wind resistance as possible. He does not have the powerful shoulders of Corey Nakatani or Jose Santos, but his smooth rhythm makes up for brute thrust when a horse is in its final drive to the finish. He keeps his competitive fire smoldering, always focused. Short of endangering another rider or presenting his horse with a ridiculous risk, Bailey will do whatever is necessary to win. When he uses the whip it is not for punishment, but more for surprise, much in the manner of a rider named Shoemaker. There are, of course, exceptions. In the final hundred yards of the 1996

Kentucky Derby, Bailey hit Grindstone with every single stride. They won the race by a nose.

"I get tears in my eyes when I watch that race," Ray York said. "You can go over it and over it, and you can't fault Jerry one single thing."

In the summer of 1996, in the midst of Cigar's record winning streak, Jorge Velasquez took Bailey aside at Arlington International Racecourse in Chicago. They had been rivals for years, especially in the early 1980s, when Velasquez was considered royalty among New York jockeys and Bailey was a pretender to the throne. Both men were in the Hall of Fame, but it was Bailey who was on top now, while Velasquez, at the age of forty-nine, was riding out the twilight of his career far from the bright lights of Broadway.

"You fit Cigar perfectly, you know that?" Velasquez said.

"Thanks," Bailey replied, "but I've always thought anybody could ride Cigar."

"No, that's not true," Velasquez shot back. "You know how to wait. You don't get excited. You're just what he needs."

If only he knew, Bailey thought. If only he knew the feeling of riding Cigar. "You never know how fast you are really going," Bailey would say, "because he never lowers his body when he accelerates, like other good horses do."

For the first time in his life, a racehorse thrilled Jerry Bailey to his bones. He dreamed Cigar dreams. He headed for Cigar's barn every day at the track. When Cigar was recovering from a bruised foot that jeopardized the beginning of his '96 campaign, Bailey would go home from the races, eat a quick supper, and return to the stables to check on the big horse. Cigar, Bailey says, is the first horse that makes him want to cry.

"Does he know me? Of course he knows me. He's too smart not to. I talk to him all the time. We strike bargains, like if he works a certain way I'll make sure he gets that extra peppermint. Sometimes he'll even get a little impatient with me. Then he let's me know, in his own way." This was after Bailey and Cigar had won sixteen straight races together.

"One morning I was working him. I wanted him to finish a little bit more than he usually does. At the head of the stretch I went to throw a new cross and got a little tangled in his mane, so I had to pull the reins through to clear them. He felt me do it and shook his head as if to say, 'What the heck are you doing back there? Just sit still!' "

In a race, Cigar is all business. After gauging the running habits of the various competition, Bailey locks his concentration on a single, insistent mantra: Do not make a mistake.

"Riding him is really very simple, though. He always wants to go. It's my job to decide when to let him go. You would not believe how hard he pulls. Sometimes my fingers go to sleep. My hands are numb."

And then there are the quiet moments. Bailey studied Cigar as a parent would study a precocious child, wondering where such ability came from and what exciting surprise would burst forth next.

"His schedule was to graze late in the morning in the yard outside Bill's barn there at Belmont. I'd always go over and just watch Cigar nibble at the grass. He'd work his way slowly over to me—I was sitting on the fence—and then he'd get in close and look up at me as if to say, 'One little nudge, pal, and you're going right over.' "

Before the winning streak began, though, Bailey harbored reasonable doubts about Cigar. He had ridden him once and lost. He was riding him in the NYRA Mile—November 26, 1994—because Mike Smith begged off Cigar to ride the race favorite, Devil His Due. The night before the race, Bailey called his friend, Gary Young, in California.

"Do you remember this horse out there?"

"Absolutely," Young replied. "Bet all I had the first time he ran. He was a great-looking horse, and I thought if he ever put it all together he could be something special. But he just never realized his potential."

"Well," Bailey came back, "I'll be testing him pretty good in the stake tomorrow."

The next night Young's phone rang. It was Bailey, and he was amazed. Cigar had humiliated good horses in the NYRA Mile, winning by seven lengths.

"I'm really surprised," Bailey said. "The way he ran today, why he hadn't done more up to now. If he keeps running like that he's going to be tough to beat wherever he goes."

If he only knew.

CHAPTER 7

PERFECTION

It is difficult to explain what happened in 1995. Perhaps it was something he ate.

Cigar would start his day with breakfast, served between three-thirty and four o'clock in the morning in a plain, dark green tub with his name written in permanent marker on the side. He would get three-quarters of a coffee can of crimped oats and a handful of sweet feed. At noon, after his work was done, he was rewarded with another three-quarters of a can of crimped oats and a quarter can of sweet feed. At dinnertime, around four o'clock, there would be a big meal, cooked up in hot water. A real soupy Bill Mott delight, it would consist of one and a quarter cans of whole oats, a half can of sweet feed, two small scoops of barley, a scoop of ground corn, a half scoop of flax seed and some bran. Cigar would plunge in up to his nostrils and eat like a man condemned.

Of course, all of Mott's horses eat pretty much the same thing. Yet only one of them earned $4,819,800 and won all ten of his races in 1995.

Maybe it was in his stars. Cigar was born in the Chinese Year of the Horse. His horoscope sign is Aries, the Ram. His ruling planet is Mars, god of combat. His gemstone is the diamond—hard, polished, exuding wealth. In *Llewellyn's Sun Sign Book*, astrologer Gloria Star writes of the Aries: "Your most intensified sense of power emerges when you're in the starting gate of an exciting challenge." What did Gloria know and when did she know it?

But Cigar was one of 44,143 thoroughbreds born in the United States and Canada in 1990. Of those, more than ten thousand hit the ground under the Aries sign. Why was he so singly blessed?

Maybe, just maybe, it was the way Cigar was constructed. A thoroughbred is rarely better than the sum of his parts. Such intangibles as aggression, desire and high tolerance for pain can sometimes overcome physical flaws. But, for the most part, the destiny of a racehorse is limited to the dimensions and alignment of his structural framework. A well-made horse will run faster, stay sounder, and last longer than a poorly made animal. There is very little romance involved.

In August of 1995, the equine conformation expert Cecil Seaman paid a visit to the Mott stables at Greentree Estates in Saratoga Springs. Seaman had been measuring horses for more than thirty years. He had a data base of more than forty-five thousand thoroughbreds. His bank of information included more than a hundred champions. It took Seaman barely five minutes with measuring tape and notepad to record some remarkable numbers. This is what he found:

Cigar had a heart girth measurement of seventy-one and three-quarter inches. From his eye to the base of his tail, he was ninety-three and a half inches long, compared to the average thoroughbred length of around ninety inches. His height from the ground to the withers at the base of the neck was just over sixteen hands, or about sixty-five inches, making Cigar, in Seaman's words, "A large horse, but not a giant." Seaman was amazed at the length of the bones in Cigar's legs, and with the perfection of their ratio. At the back of the anatomy, his hocks were twenty-seven inches from the ground, and above that his tibia was twenty-three and a half inches long, his femur was twenty-four inches, and he had a twenty-five inch span to the hip. Up front, his foreleg measured thirty-five and a half inches long and his humerus—the bone linking the shoulder to the top of the foreleg—was fourteen and a half inches.

Seaman plugged his data into a computer program. The computer was impressed. Judging leverage, power and point of gravity, Cigar's numbers crunched out an evaluation that placed this particular beast in the top three percent of the thoroughbred population. The overall grade was an A+, while his balance was nearly perfect. Seaman could barely maintain his detached, professorial demeanor as he savored each increment of Cigar's superstructure.

"He's got a phenomenal length to his femur and tibia," Seaman pointed out. "The average femur is about twenty-two inches. The average hip is twenty-three to twenty-three and a half inches. His humerus is also an inch to an inch and a half longer than average. With his shoulder and humerus, and his femur and tibia, he's got a tremendous stride. In turn, that makes him very efficient."

It was Cigar's efficiency of motion that set him apart. Jerry Bailey insisted that Cigar's feet never lifted more than a few inches off the ground. When Cigar was in full flight, Mott liked to call him a well-oiled machine, doing what it was supposed to do. Think of an engine, perfectly constructed and calibrated, humming along at eighty percent capacity and doing just as much work as another motor cranked up to full steam. With every reach and thrust of his stride, Cigar propelled himself over more terrain that an opponent who was moving his legs at a similar pace. To keep up with Cigar, no matter what the pace, other horses were always expending more energy. As Cigar increased his pace, the opposition soon reached one hundred percent effort in an attempt to keep up. But they could only sustain such output for so long. Soon they faded away, while Cigar cruised on, never reaching the depths of his full mechanical potential.

"Just once," Bailey said during the streak, "I would like to see what Cigar can do when I ask him to run as fast as he can. Maybe that time will come someday before he's through."

It certainly did not come in 1995. Cigar won all ten of his races with a combination of precision, power and predictability. From January in the tropics to a wet autumn in New York, each start offered a variation on the same relentless theme. It came as a wonderful surprise, particularly to the people in Cigar's corner, who did not dare to hold such heady expectations. In fact, they began 1995 with a variety of thorny problems that made the future downright unpredictable.

In December of 1994, Jerry Bailey led a threatened work stoppage to protest lack of sufficient insurance coverage for riders. A walkout would have played havoc with the country's top racetracks. As president of the Jockeys' Guild, Bailey was the lightning rod for criticism from owners, trainers and racetrack managements. The issue was settled at the eleventh hour, but the bitterness lingered. Bailey believed there would be retribution for his high-profile leadership. He expected nothing less than a form of blacklisting that would keep him from riding top horses for influential owners.

Allen Paulson had other worries. The annual purse earnings from his large stable of horses had plateaued at about $3 million and stayed there, in the midst of rising operating costs, through the end of 1994. Now, $3 million sounds like a lot, but even such a serious sum will disappear quickly under the pressure of six hundred horses and such expenses as commissions, taxes, training fees, insurance, farm costs, shipping, health care and personnel. The Paulson horses won just seven stakes races in all of 1994, a paltry total for an operation supposedly geared toward the top end of the sport. And to make matters even worse, Paulson's breeding operation lost its leading sire, Strawberry Road, who was disabled by illness early in 1995 and was eventually euthanized following complications.

Bill Mott, on the other hand, was coming off the best season of his career. His stable earned $7 million in purse money in 1994, good for second in the national standings behind D. Wayne Lukas. However, of that amount a healthy $2.6 million was banked by a single horse, Paradise Creek. Mott considered Paradise Creek the best horse he had ever developed from scratch. His retirement to stud duty in Japan left a gaping hole in the stable. As Mott walked up and down the shedrow of his barn at Gulfstream Park in early January of 1995, he saw no ready replacement part for the champ, and nothing on the horizon.

At the time, Cigar was enjoying life with light but steady exercise at the Payson Park training center, located about a hundred miles north of Miami in Indiantown, Florida. Back at the track, Mott was mulling over where he should run this new and improved version of a racehorse. The NYRA Mile had been impressive, no doubt. But Mott needed to see more before he was willing to feed Cigar a regular diet of Florida's toughest older horses. Cigar was still at Payson Park when, in mid-January, Mott thumbed through the Gulfstream condition book of upcoming events and stumbled upon an allowance race worth $33,000 scheduled for January 22. He liked the idea. It figured to be a nice, safe way to begin the campaign. There was a chance Cigar would be the only major stakes winner in the field. It presented Mott with an opportunity to give Cigar a conditioning race at a mile and one-sixteenth before the tough bouts ahead. Mott huddled with agent Bob Frieze, the man who booked mounts for Bailey.

"There's the race," Mott said, pointing to the date. "But don't mark it in your book." Mott and Frieze had to play the old racetrack game. If word got out that Cigar was running, other trainers might stay away and the race would have to be canceled. Frieze made the mental note in indelible ink, then spent the next week making creative excuses to other trainers who wanted Bailey for the same race.

When Cigar returned to Gulfstream Park on January 19, Mott was packing up for a trip with Tina and Brady to the highlands of Costa Rica, far from any signs of racetrack life. When Cigar ran three days later, Mott was slithering down a vine somewhere deep in the jungle, searching for lost waterfalls and a better view of the Miravalles Volcano. That evening Mott called Florida. He learned that Cigar had won easily, finishing two lengths clear of an enterprising rival named Upping the Ante. The streak was up to three.

Mott went from Costa Rica, to Florida, and then quickly to Washington, D.C., where, on the evening of January 27, he took the ballroom stage at the Washington Hilton to accept the Eclipse Award for Paradise Creek as champion turf horse of 1994. Mott retreated quietly as the attention fell upon Holy Bull, the exciting colt who reigned as America's most famous racehorse. Holy Bull was a handsome gray with a coat like a lunar landscape. He had been the dominant three-year-old of 1994. He was owned and trained by veteran Jimmy Croll, who received Holy Bull as an inheritance from a loyal patron. With his fairy tale story and his front-running flair, Holy Bull loomed as a marketing dream for the 1995 season. Racetracks all over the country were lining up to bid for an appearance by Holy Bull.

But first, Holy Bull had to deal with Cigar. Even Mott thought his big horse had a chance to run very well against the superstar. The setting at Gulfstream Park was the Donn Handicap at a mile and one-eighth on February 11. Holy Bull, carrying 127 pounds, was starting from the outside post in the field of nine, with Mike Smith in the saddle. Cigar, carrying 115 pounds, had post position number four. Before the race, Mott and Bailey talked strategy.

"I think they'll probably send the gray horse from out there," Mott said as Cigar pulled his handlers around the parade ring. "I can see you laying second."

"Fine with me," Bailey said. "We've got the speed to stay close. I should be able to get to the outside with no trouble."

To Mott's amazement, Cigar outbroke Holy Bull and led the champion into the first turn. The trainer was not a happy man. "Great. Now they've got us right where they want us," Mott grumbled. From there, Holy Bull could keep Cigar pinned to the rail, intimidating his rival while running freely on the outside. Then, just as Cigar and Holy Bull came out of the turn and onto the backstretch, Bailey heard a pop, closely followed by Mike Smith's bone-chilling scream:

"Oh no, Jerry!"

Holy Bull had ruptured the tendon below the knee of his left foreleg. In a snap, he was out of the race, being pulled to a stop by Smith. Visions of past racing disasters rippled across the country, through the thousands of fans watching the Donn on television, and through the crowd of almost nineteen thousand on the scene at Gulfstream Park. Some fought back recollections of Prairie Bayou's fatal accident in the 1993 Belmont Stakes. For others, it was October of 1990 all over again, and the sickening sight of Go for Wand breaking down in the Breeders' Cup Distaff.

"It was like someone punched me in the stomach," said

Tom Durkin, who had to react a split second after the incident. As the man who would call the race for an international audience, Durkin awoke that morning full of anticipation, ready to regale his listeners with a fresh set of Holy Bull superlatives. "All I could think of was, 'Oh no, not again.' The call of that race had more to do with what happened to Holy Bull than Cigar winning."

Cigar, suddenly alone on the lead, went on to win by five and a half lengths. The demoralized crowd barely noticed the ease with which the big brown horse was moving at the end. All eyes were on the spot in the distance where Holy Bull was being led onto a horse ambulance. Fortunately, the injury was not catastrophic. Later that evening, when the crowds had cleared from the corner of the backstretch where Jimmy Croll kept Holy Bull, Mott made the short walk from his stable to console his fellow trainer. There was not much Mott could say.

"I'm awful sorry, Jimmy. How's he doing?"

"Looks like he'll be all right, but he's through," Croll replied. "Bowed tendon. Some damage to the suspensory. Your horse ran big, huh? I guess I wasn't paying much attention."

"Yeah, he did," Mott said. "It's a little tough to enjoy a win like that, though."

Mott walked back to his barn and stopped for a moment at a stall halfway down the east side of the shedrow. Inside, Cigar was resting, shifting back and forth slightly on his back feet. His head was low, his nose pointed at the scarred wooden wall. He looked like just another horse with a full belly and a night of rest ahead. Mott thought for a minute about Holy Bull, and how quickly a dream can end. Then he focused on Cigar. He played the last half mile of the Donn again in his mind—the sight of Cigar shaking off a challenge from another horse and pulling clear to win with power to spare.

"I had a lot of friends, a couple of them real good handicappers, who thought Cigar would beat Holy Bull that day," Mott later recalled. "I prefer to say that I guess we'll never know, and that it would have been a real good horse race. But knowing what I know now, there's a very good possibility that he would have won."

Holy Bull was gone. Cigar was alone in the spotlight, if he could handle the attention. After the Donn, he ran in the $500,000 Gulfstream Park Handicap on March 5. Ten horses tried to stay with him for a mile and one-quarter, but after running a mile, when Cigar reached the lead, the last of the opposition gave up the chase. Oblivious to their distress, Cigar maintained his fluid cadence and disappeared into the distance, eventually winning by seven and a half lengths. "Visually," said Tom Durkin, "I think it was the most impressive race he ever ran. Quite literally, Bailey never asked him to run. He was like a statue on the horse. To me, that was the day he became *Cigar*. I had seen him win five straight. I had run out of things to say. It was somebody else's turn."

Much to the delight of Tim Jones, a trip to Oaklawn Park was next. The track in Hot Springs harbored fond memories for the Arkansas native. It was there, during the spring of 1984, that a twenty-year-old Jones approached Bill Mott for a job. Jones had ridden the rodeo circuit and managed a farm. He wanted to make the leap into thoroughbreds, and he wanted to work for the best. When Mott won the 1983 Oaklawn Park training title, Jones made his decision. Mott was his man. The following year Jones typed up a three-page resume and headed for the track.

Mott was supervising a set of horses early one morning, standing at the top of the backstretch chute in a steady spring rain. A noise caught his attention, and he looked around. There was a solitary figure struggling up the slippery embankment, on crutches, no less, wearing a full leg cast. It was Jones. The young man introduced himself, presented his resume, and made a pitch for a job as an exercise rider. Mott fought back a grin and looked down at the cast.

"That's not much of a recommendation," the trainer dead-panned, nodding toward the mass of plaster. "How'd it happen?"

"A yearling I was breaking at the farm flipped," Jones answered. "Busted my knee."

"Well, I guess anybody wants the job bad enough to chase me up that hill on crutches deserves a shot," Mott said. "When that thing comes off, see my assistant at Canterbury Downs."

Now Jones was back in Arkansas with Cigar for the $750,000 Oaklawn Handicap. Family and friends came from miles around to see the big horse run against a tough bunch that included Concern, winner of the 1994 Breeders' Cup Classic; Best Pal, a winner of more than $5 million;

Urgent Request, fresh from victory in the Santa Anita Handicap over Best Pal; and Silver Goblin, a local hero who had won eight straight races himself. Cigar left the gate pinned between two horses. He shook them off and settled onto the backstretch, content to race in fourth place, just behind Silver Goblin. Around the turn, he started pulling harder and harder on Bailey's arms. Bailey, who still had some pain in his chest from the accident at Keeneland three days earlier, gave Cigar some rein. Silver Goblin was about to take the lead and his jockey, Dale Cordova, was ready for the final drive. Cordova lifted his right hand and brought the whip down to smack his horse on the rump. Instead, the whip hit Cigar right across the bridge of the nose. Later, Cordova said he was sorry.

Bailey feared the worst. Sometimes, when a horse is struck in the face—accidentally or otherwise—he will pack it in and call it a day. Cigar reacted exactly the other way. Like a fighter who has been splashed with a cold bucket of water, Cigar simply shook his head. He never broke stride. In fact, Bailey got the feeling the whole thing made Cigar downright angry. The crowd of 43,111 yelled louder as Cigar passed Silver Goblin and quickly opened up. At the end, the winning margin was two and a half lengths. Cigar had passed a test for class. He was ready for whatever Mott and Paulson had in mind.

Some places carry bad memories. For Bill Mott, the word "Pimlico" triggered thoughts of a hundred grand flushed down the toilet through absolutely no fault of his own. In the spring of 1994, Mott brought Paradise Creek to the Baltimore track to run in the Dixie Handicap, a race sponsored by the Early Times whiskey company. Paradise Creek was attempting to sweep all three races in the Early Times series of top-class grass events, which began in Kentucky and would end in New York in June. The sweep would be worth a cool million to the owner of the horse. Mott's percentage would be $100,000. Sounded like a nice little college nest egg for Brady and Riley, or maybe a start on a herd of cattle in Mobridge.

The daydreaming ended on May 20, 1994, when Mott arrived at Pimlico only to discover that Richard Small, the trainer of another horse in the Dixie, had withdrawn his runner after an argument with track officials because a holding stall was not ready. Mott witnessed the hubbub from a distance. Later, it hit home hard. The loss of Small's horse cut the field to five. A minimum of six was needed to qualify for the million-dollar bonus according to the terms of the series. Paradise Creek won the Dixie, then completed his sweep later in New York. Mott was left to wonder how he would have spent his cut.

"Hell, I would have made up the stall myself if I'd have known what was going on," Mott said eight months later. It took him that long to laugh about it.

Since success is usually the best revenge, Mott did not hesitate to return to Baltimore with Cigar in the spring of 1995 for the $600,000 Pimlico Special. The race appeared ideal on paper. Cigar could take the early lead and control the pace, running as fast or slow as he pleased, leaving Bailey to dictate terms to the other riders. The main oppo-

sition was Devil His Due, who may have had a dim recollection of Cigar's fleeing tail from the NYRA Mile, and Concern,
back for more punishment after losing at Oaklawn. Concern
was trained by Richard Small.

The race was over a few steps out of the gate. Bailey let
Cigar have a bit of rein at the beginning, and he took the bait.
By the time Cigar reached the eighth pole, deep in the stretch,
he had been in front and alone for so long that crushing boredom was beginning to set in. Devil His Due, too proud to quit,
ran hard to the end and appeared to be gaining on Cigar nearing the finish line. It was an optical illusion, though. Cigar
was gearing down. The race was already won.

Cigar had his biggest audience that day. ABC Sports, in
town to prepare for the Preakness Stakes the following
Saturday, broadcast the Pimlico Special as part of its popular
"Wide World of Sports" anthology. Before that, Cigar had
been a creature of ESPN, the all-sports network available
through cable subscribers.

Mott remembers the Special, however, not because of the
coverage, nor for the purse, nor even for the ease with which
Cigar handled the challenge. He remembers the Pimlico
Special as the day Allen Paulson really started to know his
horse. Two hours before the race was to be run, Paulson disappeared from his group of friends and family in the comfortable surroundings of Pimlico's private dining room and made
the short walk to Cigar's barn with Mott. Cigar was standing
quietly, facing the back of his stall, with his hind legs done up
in ice boots. Paulson and Mott shucked their jackets and

leaned on the shedrow rail. Soon the two men fell into a rhythm of conversation they had never experienced before.

"It was like we were two stable hands, just doing the things we always do to get ready for a race," Mott recalled. The two men, thirty-one years apart in age but equals under the shedrow, talked about Cigar, and how far he had come. They talked about the future, what they could ask him to do. They talked about Cigar's occasionally troublesome hocks, being cooled down in ice as a precaution. They talked about the little things that went into the preparation for a race—the rundown bandages, the equipment, the routine. Paulson, a tireless worker who knew how to make jets fly fast and far, connected with Cigar that day as an athlete who did his job and did it well. He emerged with a typical fatherly frustration.

"He does so much for me," Paulson later said. "I sometimes wish I could do more for him. Just giving him a peppermint candy every once in awhile doesn't seem like enough."

So Paulson did the next best thing. He decided to start sharing Cigar with as many people as possible. The road show began in earnest on June 3 at Suffolk Downs, a Boston track that had been raised from the ashes of neglect. Management had invigorated the Massachusetts Handicap by contriving a bonus package at the beginning of the year designed to attract a horse who could possibly win the Gulfstream Park Handicap, the Oaklawn Handicap and the Pimlico Special. Of course, track officials thought that horse would be Holy Bull. They gladly settled for Cigar.

The race figured to be nothing more than a waltz in the park. There was no monetary incentive for other top older horses to run. So the track turned Cigar's appearance into a cultural event. He arrived with a police escort. He was lauded by local government and applauded whenever he stepped out of the barn, which was located near the center of a weather-beaten stable area that reminded Mott of the old days at Hazel Park in Detroit. On the way to the saddling paddock for the race, Cigar and Mott were greeted by a wave of cheers as they walked the length of the stretch. Homemade signs saluting Cigar appeared for the first time. It was a blue-collar crowd, puffing cigars and straining to catch a glimpse of their blue-collar hero. Cigar did not let them down. He won by four lengths over a horse named Poor But Honest.

After the Massachusetts Handicap, it was Mott's recommendation that Cigar be given a break. He had been going hard for six months. He had run at four different racetracks in four different regions of the country. The primary goal had become the Breeders' Cup Classic, to be run in late October at Belmont Park, where Mott had his main headquarters. The trainer envisioned a calm summer vacation for Cigar that would build his physical reserves in anticipation of a tough package of races at the end of the year.

Paulson suggested otherwise. He wanted to show off Cigar in California, before the same people who remembered Cigar as a mediocre grass horse. As a former member of the board of directors of Hollywood Park, Paulson leaned hard toward running in the Hollywood Gold Cup, scheduled for July 2.

When Hollywood Park increased the purse for the Gold Cup from $750,000 to $1 million, Paulson was impressed. He and Mott were in communication almost every day.

"How's Cigar doing?" Paulson was usually in his office at the Del Mar Country Club.

"Doing fine," Mott replied. "Galloped good. Seems to have handled the trip to Boston okay. I'm still not so sure he shouldn't have a break, though, before the fall."

"Well," Paulson said, "other than that, is there any reason he shouldn't run in the Gold Cup?"

"No, not really, other than the fact that a lot of good horses from back here sometimes don't run so good out there. I took a mare named Heatherten out there in 1984 for the Vanity Handicap. She had won seven races in a row and was maybe the best mare in the country. But that day she didn't run a jump. Ran so bad I couldn't believe it, and I never figured out why."

"Well, maybe so," Paulson said. "But this is Cigar. And I've always felt that the reward is only as great as the risk."

Other than his own gut feeling—magnified by the lingering trauma of the Heatherten experience—Mott could not give Paulson a good reason not to run in the Hollywood Gold Cup. Early on the morning of July 1, Cigar was vanned from Belmont Park to Kennedy International Airport, then flown to the West Coast via Chicago in the company of Tim Jones and Juan Campuzano. There was an hour delay along the way and a few bumps in the weather. By the time Cigar arrived at Hollywood Park, he looked jet-lagged and drawn.

There was no official greeting, no police escort and only a few people from track management on hand to meet the van as Cigar walked down the ramp. In Boston, Cigar was greeted by fanfare and adulation. In Los Angeles, he was like a thief sneaking back into town.

The local reaction was skeptical. The last time Californians had seen Cigar in the flesh he was finishing up the track in the 1993 Hollywood Derby. At that point, his record in California was two wins in nine starts. What was the big deal? So the horse knocks off a few easy pots in the East? Trainer Bobby Frankel, freshly elected to the Hall of Fame, said bring him on. "I'll beat him with Tinners Way," he vowed. The Southern California handicappers were nearly unanimous in picking against Cigar. They went for Concern, who had come West after the Pimlico Special to win the Californian Stakes impressively. They touted Tinners Way, even without Frankel's promise. Or they liked Urgent Request, the Santa Anita Handicap winner who had been so thoroughly beaten by Cigar at Oaklawn Park. Even Best Pal, age seven and past his prime, was preferred to Cigar.

Paulson thought he was seeing things the morning of the Gold Cup when he turned to the sports section of his Los Angeles *Times* and perused the Hollywood Park handicap consensus. There, in black and white, was a sight he thought he would never see. After toting up the selections, Cigar was not among the first three picks in the race. Unbelievable, Paulson said. What part of perfect did they not understand? Was it the eight straight victories, six in a row in 1995, four of them major events? Or did they not notice that he won them all by daylight margins?

The bad vibes carried into the paddock before the race. As Best Pal paraded in the ring he was cheered. When Cigar walked around, calmly eyeing the railbirds with his warm right eye, they booed and shouted insults. Suddenly, Cigar was wearing the black hat. He was heavily favored by the fans in the betting, but their hearts strayed elsewhere. Even Bailey started to waver. Driving to the track for the Gold Cup, his friend Gary Young picked up an attitude that read, "If they're ever going to beat him, today would be the day." Young, who knew the local horses like the back of his hand, had to say something.

"Look," Young said as Bailey headed for the jockeys' room, "you're on the best horse this country has seen in at least ten years. Take no prisoners."

It was a massacre. Bailey felt a power from Cigar like never before. Breaking from the inside post, he had hoped to gradually ease to the outside around the first turn, and from there stalk the leaders until giving Cigar his head with three-eighths of a mile to run. Everything went perfectly until, about two hundred yards into the race, Cigar was struck in the face by a balled up clod of hard-packed sandy loam. His reaction was typical L.A. If something happens on the freeway, get angry and look for someone to blame.

Bailey felt Cigar chew down on the bit and accelerate. Suddenly, he was running up the heels of the three horses in front as they rounded the first turn. Bailey angled Cigar to the outside, losing ground but preventing disaster. As the leaders completed the turn and began the long run down the backstretch, Cigar was on the far outside, still pulling at Bailey's arms. The rider was losing all feeling in his hands. The left rein had cut off the circulation to his fingers. Outweighed by nearly half a ton and in no mood to argue, Bailey surrendered, and Cigar began pulling away from the field. Tinners Way emerged from the pack to make a respectable run for second place, but he was a helpless three and a half lengths behind the winner. Up in the stands, Bobby Frankel shook his head and delivered a brief but eloquent concession speech: "That horse is too #%&@! good."

Mott let loose a deep sigh of relief. Now it was time for a rest. Cigar returned to Belmont Park, where Mott kept him in light training. Three weeks after the Gold Cup, Cigar was treated for some minor inflammation in his right front ankle. Slowly, it returned to normal. Mott attributed the damage to the wear and tear of the tough campaign. A complete set of X-rays revealed nothing else amiss. Cigar was able to return to more serious training in mid-August at Saratoga. Then it was back to Belmont Park, where Cigar had a date in the Woodward Stakes at a mile and one-eighth on September 16.

Jack Nicholson was in the crowd that day, smoking a great big cigar. Anyone who had one was wearing their specially designed Laura Pearson ties adorned with smoldering stogies. Mott knew Cigar was ready, because a few days before the race the trainer had made the mistake of bringing him to the paddock for a "schooling" session, designed to reacclimate

Cigar to the sights and sounds and smells of the racetrack in the afternoon. After all, it had been more than two months since he had raced.

But Cigar's memory was just fine. The session in the Belmont paddock tripped all of his competitive switches. He felt all dressed up with no place to run. Stimulated by the experience, he was on a slow boil all the way back to the barn. Once at home he took out his frustrations on his stall like a grounded teenage boy. Basically, he trashed his room. Mott promised himself never again. Never take Cigar to the racetrack unless you plan to turn him loose.

There was not much depth to the field for the Woodward, although Schossberg had just won the Philip Iselin Handicap at Monmouth Park—beating good old Poor But Honest—and Star Standard was among the best of the current three-year-old generation. The race unfolded to perfection, as far as Bailey was concerned, until jockey Pat Day let Star Standard float Cigar very wide around the final turn into the stretch. It did not matter. Once they straightened for the final run to the finish, Cigar cruised clear to win by two and three-quarter lengths. Jack Nicholson and his cigar joined the Paulsons in the winner's circle.

Cigar's winning streak had reached ten in a row. He was edging into special historical company. Sysonby, the first great American horse of the twentieth century, won ten straight in 1904 and 1905. Count Fleet won ten in a row between October of 1942 and June of 1943, including the American Triple Crown. The great filly Ruffian was untouchable in her first ten races before suffering a fatal injury in the 1975 match race against Foolish Pleasure. Spectacular Bid, the horse to whom Cigar was being closely compared in substance and style, closed out his career winning his final ten races, nine of them during his perfect 1980 campaign.

D. Wayne Lukas, always outspoken, thought he had the horse to put the brakes on the streak, and he said so, loud and clear. The apple of his eye was Thunder Gulch, winner of the 1995 Kentucky Derby and Belmont Stakes. In the months following the Derby and Belmont, the short, broad-beamed chestnut had traveled far and wide, winning the Swaps Stakes in California, the Travers Stakes at Saratoga and the Kentucky Cup Classic at Turfway Park in northern Kentucky. Now it was time for the Jockey Club Gold Cup at Belmont Park. Now it was time to face Cigar.

Paulson respected Thunder Gulch, but after awhile he got tired of listening to Lukas. On Gold Cup day, it was time to put up or pipe down. "I've got quite a bit of money here," Paulson said, patting his pocket, when he spotted Lukas. "How about you and me have a little side bet on this race." Lukas smiled and decided to let Thunder Gulch do the talking. Paulson shrugged and put his wallet away. Cigar took over from there.

Star Standard was back for another try, going a mile and one-quarter this time, and he was on the lead through the first part of the race. The ground was wet from recent rains and a little sticky as it dried out during the day. Cigar had never competed over such a surface, and Bailey sensed his discomfort. He fed Cigar a little slack as they entered the far turn, where they encountered Thunder Gulch. Cigar ran alongside the Derby winner for a few strides, then lost interest. With ruthless efficiency, he dismissed Thunder Gulch as a minor nuisance and went after Star Standard, a far more interesting prey.

Once again, Star Standard carried Cigar far out into the center of the track. Down on the inside, a horse named Unaccounted For left Thunder Gulch struggling in his wake and made a mad dash after the leaders. Bailey shook loose from Star Standard and smacked Cigar with his whip. Through the final two hundred yards, Unaccounted For reached as hard as he could and kept Cigar in his sights. But Cigar was just cruising, running in that geared down zone so impossible to penetrate. At the finish, Bailey allowed Unaccounted For to close within a length. But there was never any danger of an upset, and the rest of the runners finished far, far behind—including Thunder Gulch.

"I guess Lukas got a little smoke in his eyes," Paulson cracked after watching Thunder Gulch finish a distant fifth. As it turned out, the Derby winner suffered a hairline fracture in the cannon bone of his left foreleg. He was retired from racing.

Few harbored delusions that Thunder Gulch would have upset Cigar under any circumstances that day. There was the lingering thought, however, that Cigar's failure to dominate the Jockey Club Gold Cup in his normal fashion had revealed a chink in his armor. Was the wet, sticky track a problem for the big horse with the giant stride? If so, what would happen in the Breeders' Cup Classic if the track came up less than fast and dry? The streak had reached eleven. The Classic, with its purse of $3 million, would be a magnet for every good dirt horse in the world. They would all be gunning for Cigar. And Mott could not do a thing about the weather.

As the Breeders' Cup approached—and the rains continued to fall in New York—Cecil Seaman paid a visit to the Mott stable to pay his respects and, at the same time, deliver his analysis of Cigar's measurements taken two months earlier in Saratoga. Mott gave the numbers a quick look, and then his eyes fell upon a comment at the bottom of the page. Based upon Cigar's superior balance and conformation, Seaman was comfortable in predicting that the horse would be at his best on either a fast track—no surprise there—or on a sloppy track.

Let it rain.

SUMMIT

Bill Mott awoke from a fitful sleep. Beside him Tina stirred and sighed. Mott blinked into the darkness of the bedroom and picked up right where his agitated mind had left off. Hives and mud. Mud and hives. The rain had stopped, for now. The medication had worked, thank goodness. The swelling was down. Cigar could train. Mott looked at the bedside clock. Might as well get up, he thought. No sense in lying here wide awake. It was Monday morning, and for most of the families of Garden City it was back to work and back to school. For Bill Mott, it was back to Belmont Park, where Breeders' Cup week was about to begin.

Less than a half hour later, Mott's brown Lincoln LSC crunched to a stop on the gravel outside his barn on the Belmont backstretch. The trainer made a beeline for stall three, where Cigar stood serenely beneath the light of a two-hundred watt bulb. He looked more like a racehorse again and less like a pastry. Cigar's lips were still puffy, and there was some trace of swelling around his eyes. But for the most part the dramatic disfigurement of the previous day was gone.

As the final countdown to the twelfth running of the $10-million Breeders' Cup extravaganza commenced, Mother Nature decided to play havoc with both star and stage. The Breeders' Cup—with its seven races of championship quality and its four and a half hours of network television exposure—was scheduled for Saturday, October 28. The climactic moment of the day would occur in the $3-million Breeders' Cup Classic, when Cigar would face the most difficult challenge of his life. His perfect season would be on the line with an audience of millions watching. The people at NBC Sports were praying for Cigar to make it a memorable day. So far, nothing much had gone right.

The Breeders' Cup Preview program on October 7 attracted only 15,457 fans to Belmont Park. Perhaps Cigar wasn't such a great box office draw after all. On top of that, his one-length victory over Unaccounted For that day in the Jockey Club Gold Cup was being criticized as a substandard, worrisome performance. Speculation raced through the news mill: Was Cigar off form? Was the muddy track to blame? What would happen when he faced a stronger field in the Classic?

Two weeks later, on October 21, it rained so hard on Long Island that the racing program at Belmont Park had to be canceled. More storms were predicted for the week ahead, including a powerful squall that was due to hit Long Island on either Friday night or Saturday, the day of the Breeders' Cup. Track management and Breeders' Cup officials drew up contingency plans, which included a cancellation and rescheduling of the entire event.

The grass in the broad, fenced yard outside the Mott shedrow was still quite damp on the morning of Sunday, October 22, when Cigar was led out for his daily graze. With a handler at each side of his head, the big horse picked and nibbled, searching for sweet clover amongst the blades of stringy fescue.

Less than an hour later, Cigar was in his stall when Juan Campuzano noticed something wrong. Cigar's sleek brown coat, normally so firm and tight over his well developed muscles, was suddenly puffing up in pillow-sized welts. Soon he was swollen from head to tail with a raging case of hives. He could have swallowed a poisonous weed or ingested a toxic insect. Jim Hunt, Mott's stable vet, was on the scene immediately, and Cigar was injected with a fast-acting anti-inflammatory. As a further precaution, Mott had Cigar's stall completely cleaned and bedded with fresh straw. The trainer and his staff spent the rest of the day at the barn monitoring Cigar's progress. By that evening, most of the swelling had subsided. It could have been much, much worse.

Fortunately, Cigar was not debilitated by the ordeal. In fact, he was as physically fit as he had ever been in his life. The Jockey Club Gold Cup did nothing to deplete his reserves. His daily gallops since the race had been strong and purposeful. On October 19, he had worked a smooth six furlongs on the Belmont main track. After recovering from the attack of hives, the only formal piece of conditioning that remained before the Breeders' Cup was his traditional five-furlong exercise three days before the race. Between Monday and Wednesday, Mott gauged Cigar carefully and was amazed. It was almost as if the minor physical trauma had released a wave of invigorating endorphins. Cigar's

Wednesday morning workout, with Jerry Bailey aboard, left both the rider and the trainer full of confidence. Cigar seemed unfazed by the lingering dampness of the track. He finished the work with the same distracted air of an athlete who was bored by practice. He was ready for the game.

The other players had assembled at Belmont Park. They came from as far away as Canada, California and Great Britain. It was worth the journey. The Classic offered a first prize of $1,560,000 to the winning owner. The winning jockey stood to earn $156,000 for about two minutes of work. The winning trainer would take home a similar prize. The winning horse would get the same meal that night as he got every night, while his name would go down in racing history as the winner of America's richest horse race.

The owners of these horses each paid $60,000 in entry fees for the privilege of competing against Cigar. They could afford it, and their horses, for the most part, had earned the right to appear alongside Cigar in the Classic. The cast included:

Khalid Abdullah, a member of the royal family of Saudi Arabia, London businessman and proprietor of one of the world's largest and most successful thoroughbred breeding and racing operations. Tinners Way, the son of Secretariat who chased Cigar in California, was Abdullah's only chance to win an elusive Breeders' Cup event after seventeen unsuccessful tries between 1984 and 1994.

Josephine Abercrombie, the flamboyant Texas oil heiress, accomplished show horse rider, thoroughbred breeder and boxing promoter. She was known as much for her fighters as for her horses until Peaks and Valleys, her colt in the Classic, came along to be one of the top three-year-olds of the 1995 season.

Burt Bacharach, the Oscar, Emmy and Grammy Award winning composer. He wrote "Raindrops Keep Falling on My Head," among hundreds of other popular tunes, and prayed for the song to come true on Classic day for his elegant black colt Soul of the Matter, who loved to run in the mud.

William Condren, a Harvard educated lawyer and Wall Street investor, and his partner Joseph Cornacchia, whose publishing and printing companies helped give the world Pictionary and Trivial Pursuit. They were taking on Cigar for the third straight time with stubborn Star Standard.

Irv and Marjorie Cowan, who won a Breeders' Cup race in 1993 with the champion filly Hollywood Wildcat. Irv Cowan made his money in Florida luxury apartments, shopping malls and hotels. They were represented in the Classic by French Deputy, a gorgeous chestnut colt who had lost only one race in his short career.

John Werner Kluge, founder of Metromedia, ranked by *Forbes* magazine as the third richest man in America in 1995, and owner of the 11,500-acre Morven Stud in Virginia. His colors had come closest to upsetting Cigar when Unaccounted For finished second in the Jockey Club Gold Cup, which gave the four-year-old colt every right to try again.

Robert Meyerhoff, a builder and developer from Maryland, whose farm was only a few miles down the road from Country Life, where Cigar was born. Meyerhoff won the 1994 Classic with Concern, the little brown colt who was back to defend his crown. But Concern was zero-for-three against Cigar.

Sheikh Mohammed and his brother, Sheikh Maktoum, who raced together under the Godolphin Stable name. Sheikh Mohammed was on hand with Halling, a lissome, businesslike colt who had strung together eight consecutive victories between campaigns in England and Dubai. The Classic was one of the few major international events Sheikh Mohammed had failed so far to win.

Virginia Kraft Payson, a former sports writer and widow of Charles Shipman Payson. She bred and raced a European Horse of the Year, St. Jovite, and earlier campaigned Travers Stakes winner Carr de Naskra. Payson also owned the Payson Park training center in Florida where her Classic horse, L'Carriere, had trained the previous winter alongside Cigar.

Robert Perez, an Argentine dreamer who made his fortune in New York construction. His Classic entrant was Jed Forest, an overmatched colt who had been a champion in Panama. Jed Forest's only prior brush with fame came after he nearly got in Cigar's way coming to a stop after finishing a distant sixth in the Jockey Club Gold Cup.

In the face of Cigar's record against all those who had come before, there was no real reason to expect an upset. He was running his favorite distance of a mile and one-quarter. He was carrying the same weight as the other older horses in the field, and just five more pounds—126 to 121—than the sprinkling of three-year-old challengers. The muddy track created a shadow of a doubt, but it was a condition they all had to face.

A brief, dramatic storm dumped about an inch of rain on the area surrounding Belmont Park on the night before the Classic. Then it moved on, leaving a sky filled with towering cumulus clouds and peek-a-boo sunshine by the time the Breeders' Cup program got under way at 11:55 Saturday morning. The Classic was still more than three hours away, but no more rain was in sight. The track had been packed tightly the night before with heavy equipment, leaving a hard base topped by a layer of slippery mud. Midway through the program, a majestic rainbow appeared in the sky to the north.

The optimists among Cigar's opposition savored the sight as a benevolent omen in the face of overwhelming odds. If there was any strand of hope to their chances against Cigar, however, it came not from rainbows and good luck charms, but from the history of the Classic itself. For despite its reputation as the ultimate proving ground for the world's best horses on the dirt, the Classic's previous eleven runnings were littered with shock waves and stunning surprises. From the very beginning, the absurd and unexpected became the norm.

In 1984, when the Breeders' Cup made its debut at Hollywood Park, Wild Again was ignored at odds of 31-to-1 in the Classic, yet he beat favorites Slew o' Gold, Gate Dancer and Desert Wine. In 1985 the winner was Proud Truth, a capable three-year-old who had never run such a brilliant race before or after his Classic. In 1986 the Classic was billed as a Horse of the Year duel between Precisionist and Turkoman; but the horse all alone at the end was Skywalker, running the best race of his life at odds of 10-to-1.

Jerry Bailey, quietly preparing for the ride on Cigar, knew better than anyone not to take the Classic for granted. The first time he rode in the race he finished last. The second time his horse could not finish at all. Finally, in 1991, he hooked up with a tough gray horse named Black Tie Affair. Together they led all the way to beat a field that included Kentucky Derby winners Unbridled and Strike the Gold. So began the Bailey Era.

In the 1993 Breeders' Cup Classic at Santa Anita, Bailey landed on an inconsistent French invader named Arcangues, who had never before run on a surface other than grass. Afterwards, as he was bringing the horse back from their two-length victory, Bailey asked the outrider at his side, "How do you pronounce this horse's name, anyway?" The answer was "ahr-KONG" and the payoff on a two-dollar bet at Santa Anita was $269.20.

Bailey's expectations were slightly higher in 1994 at Churchill Downs when he rode Concern, a late-running colt who did not arrive in Kentucky until late on the night before the race. Obviously, Concern slept on the van. He and Bailey slipped through the field of fourteen to beat the favorite, Tabasco Cat, by a neck at odds of 7-to-1.

Bailey spent the early part of the 1995 Breeders' Cup program testing the traction of the racetrack, while his mounts ran hot and cold. He started the day winning the Juvenile Fillies with the popular filly My Flag, a daughter of two champions. In the Sprint—a million-dollar race lasting less than seventy seconds—Bailey's horse finished last. He was last again in the Distaff while riding Vinista for Madeleine and

Allen Paulson. In the Breeders' Cup Mile Bailey neither learned a thing nor earned a dime. It was run on the deep, swampy grass and Bailey's horse finished next-to-last. Then, in the Juvenile for two-year-olds, Bailey finished third on Editor's Note, a massive colt with a giant stride who seemed uncertain about the ground beneath his feet. Even with Cigar's more efficient stride, Bailey could not be sure how he would react to the surface.

That morning, Jim Bayes had done what he always did with Cigar's hind shoes. After pulling them off he tapped the ends slightly downward and toward the inside, then nailed them back in place with a few swift, precise strokes of his small hammer. The angle provided what blacksmiths called a "trailer," which had the same effect as attaching a mud caulk, cleat or "sticker" that provided a bit more traction on slippery, muddy ground. Bayes pointed out that trailers leveled the back of the shoe with the front toe grab. They were considerably different from the aluminum racing plates known as turn-downs, which were longer than the standard shoe and featured a dramatic downward angle of the tips. Turn-downs were illegal.

And what Cigar did to his opposition was a crime.

The Belmont saddling ring was packed to the rim as Campuzano and Tim Jones led Cigar up the ramp of the tunnel from the backstretch and into Belmont's picturesque, tree-lined paddock. Simon Bray was alongside, while Mott trailed the pack, chomping on a stick of gum and slogging through the mud in his rainy day Wal-Mart shoes. Madeleine Paulson appeared with her latest hat to end all hats, while Allen stood beside Mott in the saddling enclosure and calmly admired his horse.

"I'm more excited than nervous," Paulson confessed as Mott smoothed the Breeders' Cup saddle towel with the white "10" on a regal purple field. "I was in some pretty hairy situations as a test pilot, where you had to act without thinking or you were finished. Now that was something to get nervous about."

Madeleine Paulson felt otherwise. "I don't understand why it gets harder every time rather than easier," she said, forcing a brave smile. "I suppose it's because the expectations for him are so much greater every time he runs."

So was the scrutiny. Mott had barely set the saddle and checked the girths when he was informed that Cigar would need to submit to an inspection of his shoes. At first Mott could not believe his ears. Then he went quietly ballistic. "I don't think I've ever seen him angrier," Jones said later. While the other ten horses circled under the trees with their riders aboard, Cigar stood and fidgeted as Tom Goettsheim, the official farrier, examined the racing plates on his hind feet. Goettsheim reported that they were trailers, not turn-downs, as someone had suggested to the stewards.

That someone turned out to be Bobby Frankel, the razor-sharp trainer of Tinners Way, who caught a glimpse of Cigar's hind shoes as he entered the paddock. Gamesmanship? Perhaps. Mott called it a desperate tactic by a man who knew he had no chance to win. Frankel defended his claim. "They looked like turn-downs to me," Frankel said later. "I don't have to apologize doing that. I'm looking out for my owner and the chances of his horse in the race." Tinners Way was one of six horses in the field whose shoes had been modified with mud caulks.

Mott waited for the crowd to disperse and then had a few harsh words with officials. "He has been wearing these same shoes all year long," the trainer insisted. "He was shod this way for the Woodward. He was shod this way for the Gold Cup. I can't believe you'd make an issue of this today." With that, Mott rushed out of the paddock and up to the box seats, where the Paulsons and their party had gathered. Finally—after the shoes, the hives, the rain, and the travel far and wide during a season that no one would soon forget—it was time for Cigar to take his place at the top of the game. It was exactly one year to the day that his winning streak had begun.

The starting gate for the mile and one-quarter course at Belmont Park sits at the beginning of the clubhouse turn. The horses are faced with a short straightaway and then the remainder of the left-handed turn onto the backstretch. The higher the number in the gate, the worse the position. Cigar was in post number ten. With a couple of light taps fore and aft from Bailey's whip, the big horse entered the starting stall at 3:08 p.m., shifted his back feet into position and stared straight ahead. Jed Forest was the last to load in stall number eleven. There was a five-second pause while Robert Duncan, the Belmont starter, satisfied himself that all the horses were ready. Then Duncan pushed the button that cut the magnetic current holding the stall doors together, and eleven gates clattered open. The Breeders' Cup Classic was under way.

Great races—like great plays—have three unforgettable acts. Act I of the 1995 Classic belonged to Star Standard. He was fastest off the blocks and led the field down the short chute to the turn, while L'Carriere and Cigar joined in close pursuit. French Deputy, Unaccounted For, Peaks and Valleys and Halling were clustered in the next flight. The rest kept their distance.

After less than a quarter of a mile was run, it became apparent that some of the horses were uncomfortable with the muddy ground. Their jockeys could tell the difference in their hands. The reins fell slack. Strides were choppy, irregular. It was a helpless feeling, and there was nothing they could do about it. But even if their horses were handling the mud, one look at Bailey and their hearts sank. As Star Standard led the field down the backstretch and into the distant turn, Cigar was waging a war of isometric aggression with his jockey. It was Bailey's plan to wait as long as he could to give Cigar free rein. On this day, Cigar wanted to fly like the wind from the moment he left the starting gate. But to Bailey, that did not necessarily mean Cigar would be able to grip the mud at full speed later on.

To conserve Cigar's strength, Bailey used what leverage he could to restrain him. While the other riders stayed low, their knees bent and moving in rhythm, Bailey thrust his feet forward in the stirrups and leaned back hard against the bit in Cigar's mouth. Cigar arched his neck and indulged his jockey for awhile. But soon Bailey realized that this was an argument he could never win. After five furlongs—halfway through the race—Bailey's arms began to tingle. He remembered the Hollywood Gold Cup when his hand went numb and he could barely grip the whip. He thought, "What the hell. Let's go."

Up in the stands, Mott saw what was happening through his binoculars. Cigar was launching himself through the mud with incredible force. The other riders were already urging their horses to keep up, while Bailey sat still as stone. Mott pressed the binoculars hard against his glasses and whispered, "Why not?" as if he were answering Bailey's decision to unleash the big horse once and for all. There was nearly half a mile left to run in the Classic. But it was no longer a horse race. It was becoming a work of art.

High atop the Belmont stands, announcer Tom Durkin was in the midst of his call for a worldwide television audience. He already had described seven of Cigar's eleven straight winning races, so he knew what to expect. His challenge was to make his blow-by-blow report of the Classic sound fresh, yet he realized he had to take his cue from Cigar. "I knew what Bailey wanted to do," Durkin said. "That was to hold, hold, hold, and then finally let him go, somewhere over there on the turn. I wanted to hit it right when he made that move and punch the crowd up. As it turned out"—Durkin chuckled at the recollection—"Cigar got a little bit ahead of me."

As theater, it worked. Act II was over when the field reached the far turn. Act III had begun. Bailey let a bit of rein slip through his aching grip and Cigar accelerated instantly. He pulled alongside Star Standard and L'Carriere, but their association lasted only a few strides. Like a missile emerging from a prairie silo, Cigar's head and flying mane crested Star Standard's gold shadow roll and L'Carriere's white blinkers. Then came his shoulder, his flank…and then he was fully exposed to the view from both television and stands.

Durkin was busy accounting for the runners far behind Cigar when the explosion occurred. His reaction was swift:

"…a break of three to Jed Forest, followed by Tinners Way. Concern is still last. Three furlongs to go—CIGAR! CIGAR MAKES HIS MOVE, AND HE SWEEPS TO THE LEAD WITH A DRAMATIC RUSH AS JERRY BAILEY TURNS HIM LOOSE!"

The crowd responded with a deep, throaty roar, undoubtedly similar to the sound the Christians heard from Roman throngs just as the lions were set loose in the Coliseum. Bailey, free now to ride like the wind, pulled his whip from his left hand to his right, twirled it into position and smacked Cigar once on the side of his massive rump. Cigar took the signal and reached to a full extension of his greedy stride. Bailey stretched back for another whack and peeked under his arm. L'Carriere was still in pursuit, refusing to quit. Bailey took two more slaps at Cigar and then switched the whip back to the left hand, putting it away for the day. Together they glided under the line, two and a half-lengths in the clear, as Durkin sealed the moment with an operatic climax belted out to the back of the house:

"And here he is—the unconquerable, invincible, unbeatable Cigar!" It was impromptu poetry.

"You throw a lot into your brain," Durkin explained. "And whatever's there you hope you can retrieve. Those were all different words I could have used. As it turned out, I used them all."

L'Carriere, proud to the end, finished second. Unaccounted For was a close third, and Soul of the Matter entered the picture late to take fourth. The rest were strewn far behind. The Paulsons and the Motts hugged and hollered and headed down the winding clubhouse stairs to greet their champion as he returned. Out on the track, Simon Bray wiped a tear of joy and reached up to embrace Bailey's leg. Tim Jones and Juan Campuzano, wearing matching smiles, secured Cigar with their shanks and took control. Mott grinned up at his jockey and then, out of trainer's habit, glanced down at Cigar's legs—the remarkably made legs that had just carried Cigar to the fastest Classic in the history of the Breeders' Cup. They were perfect.

Three hours after the race, as darkness descended upon the Belmont backstretch, Mott stood at Cigar's stall. It was quiet again. Jones and Bray were finishing the evening chores. A low-key beer bash had wrapped up out back, and now Mott and Tina were ready to head for a post Breeders' Cup party out on the island. The trainer lingered and let his mind wander.

"When I was growing up, the great horses were Buckpasser and Damascus," Mott said. "I'd follow them every week in *The Blood-Horse*. It seemed like they were always on the cover. They became kind of the standard for me of what a really good horse could do. When Secretariat came along I was training a few horses in Detroit. I guess I thought I was pretty smart, because when I watched him in the post parade for the Belmont Stakes I told anyone who would listen that he looked dead lame. Then he won by thirty-one lengths. I guess I didn't know as much as I thought I did.

"Now sometimes I'll wake up, or I'll stop and think, 'I'm training Cigar.' It's a tremendous responsibility. And it's a tremendous privilege, too. I always like to remind the people who work for me just how special it is for us to be around this particular horse at this time in history."

CHAPTER 9

ARMAGEDDON

Cigar was not a happy horse. Downright grouchy, as a matter of fact. Standing at the back of his air-conditioned stall, his feet nestled deep in the thick straw bedding, he stared at the freshly painted white wall just inches from his nose. His manner was sullen. He was in no mood to eat. His coat had lost some of its burnished glow. It was a sure sign things were not quite right.

Cigar wanted to be left alone, but now there were sounds coming from the men standing at his stall door. Their voices, and their smells, were vaguely familiar. Cigar turned his head and regarded the men with his mean left eye. Then he turned away, preferring to contemplate the wall.

"Did he leave any yesterday?" The soft, flat baritone belonged to Bill Mott.

"Yeah, a little, kind of like before," Tim Jones answered.

Mott had not seen Cigar for a week, not since he had watched the big horse loaded onto a traveling pallet and tucked into the bowels of an Emery Worldwide DC-8 cargo jet at South Florida's Fort Lauderdale Airport, not far from the Mott stable at Gulfstream Park. A refueling stop at Shannon Airport near Dublin, Ireland, was delayed an hour by the revels of St. Patrick's Day. Finally, eighteen hours after departure, Cigar completed his journey to the other side of the world.

Now he was in Dubai, training in a strange land on deep, sandy ground. And he was not a happy horse.

"How about Snowball?" Mott asked Jones. Snowball was Cigar's twelve-year-old traveling companion, a genial white pony with a full figure and an appetite to match.

"He's doing a lot better," Jones said. "Back on his feed."

Mott felt slightly relieved. Snowball was hit with a bout of "shipping sickness" and spiked a fever after arriving in Dubai. "If Snowball was leaving grain I guess it can happen to any horse."

Of course, nothing like Dubai had ever happened before. Cigar was in the Middle East on a mission so outrageous, so seemingly impossible, that the mere thought of his participation in the first running of the Dubai World Cup—a race worth $4-million in total prize money—was enough to stagger the sensible mind.

After ending his 1995 campaign with a win in the Breeders' Cup Classic, Cigar wintered at the Payson Park training center in Florida. The 1996 season would commence on February 10 at Gulfstream Park in the Donn Handicap. On the night before the Donn, however, the Cigar crew was three thousand miles away, spending the evening as the center of attention at the Eclipse Awards Dinner in San Diego, California. Paulson, Bailey and Mott all won individual Eclipse Awards, attaching themselves firmly to the coattails of Cigar, who was overwhelmingly acclaimed 1995 Horse of the Year. After the dinner, they jumped in Paulson's Gulfstream IV and flew overnight to Miami—crossing over checkpoint "cigar"—arriving in time for the Donn the following day.

This would be no soft spot for a safe return, however. No one was anxious to cut the champ any slack. Seven horses ran against Cigar in the Donn, including Heavenly Prize, the five-year-old mare who had won nine times in top company, and Wekiva Springs, an athletic gray from another corner of the Bill Mott stable who was rapidly becoming a star in his own right.

When the horses were called for the race, Juan Campuzano slipped on the red vest with the big "1" emblazoned in white, smoothed his hair and set his handsome Stetson in place. It was time to lead Cigar down the stable road to the holding area before the Donn. Moments later, as Campuzano and Cigar walked alongside the outer rail of the homestretch, heading for the saddling paddock, the applause and cheers slowly began to build. Cigar cocked his head and took in the sights. It had been more than three months since he had been subjected to such an experience. Embedded memory was starting to kick in. This was not the usual leg-stretching exercise. This was the other thing.

By the time Mott got Cigar's personalized saddlecloth in place and the saddle tightly cinched, the big horse was getting edgy. Cigar arched his neck, flexed his shoulders and hips, and began to prance as he was led into the walking ring. Campuzano got help from Ralph Nicks, who held fast to a strap on the other side of Cigar's head. Bailey emerged from the jockeys' room, took one look at Cigar and said to himself, "He's ready."

He was. There was a moment as the horses entered the first

turn, in front of the clubhouse, when Bailey had to steer Cigar out of a potentially troublesome traffic jam. Cigar responded like a well-tuned V-8, and from there it was just a matter of how hard Bailey wanted to ride and how fast he wanted Cigar to run. Cigar was carrying 128 pounds—including 109 pounds of jockey and the rest in saddle and lead weights—the most he had ever carried before. Bailey saw no reason to ask Cigar for his finest hour. Certainly not so early in the year, when a bounty of races loomed on the horizon like rich piles of gold and silver.

At one point on the final turn, Wekiva Springs tried to run with his stablemate. Bailey humored the other horse for awhile—the crowd roared when they saw the gray—and then he gave Cigar a light nudge at the base of the neck. It was all the signal Cigar needed to run faster, then even faster, until he was comfortably in front of Wekiva Springs. At the end of the race, Bailey was bent over double and frozen in place, holding the reins hard against the D-bit clenched in Cigar's strong mouth. The official winning margin was two lengths.

Cigar's efficient return in the Donn set up a number of choices. The $1-million Santa Anita Handicap on March 2 appeared to be the next logical step. The Dubai World Cup, fraught with unknowns, was scheduled for March 27. Mott and Paulson felt the genuine lure of both events. The race at Santa Anita was rich with history and prestige—not to mention a first prize of $600,000 and a leg up on a $2-million bonus inspired by Cigar. The race in Dubai was a window to a brave new world, but there was no guarantee Cigar could even recover from such an experience.

"Can we make both races?" Paulson wondered.

"It's possible," Mott said, hedging his bet.

"Well," Paulson said. "If it's possible, he's the horse who could do it."

Mott did not disagree. He knew, though, that Cigar would need to be at his best to win both. The Donn provided the perfect preparation for the California race; but there was the very real possibility that the Santa Anita Handicap would drain Cigar's physical reserves, right on the eve of a long stretch of air travel to Dubai.

Ten days later, none of that mattered. On the morning of February 21, just before he was scheduled to gallop, Cigar was favoring his right front foot. Mott and his veterinarian, Dr. Jim Prendergast, discovered the evidence of a bruise. The foot was already susceptible to injury, having sustained a quarter crack the previous November, after the Breeders' Cup. A weakness in the hoof wall had been detected back then, but with no racing on the horizon, Mott had time to let the injury heal without heroic measures. This new problem threatened Cigar's appearance in not only the Santa Anita Handicap, but the Dubai World Cup as well.

Mott put in a call to Jim Bayes, who dropped what he was doing at Oaklawn Park and headed for the airport. But his flight was fogged in. Mott learned of the delay and decided he could not wait any longer. Cigar needed his help. An accomplished farrier himself—the legacy of his younger days on the South Dakota circuit and his apprenticeship with Jack Van Berg—Mott strapped on his smithy's apron, planted himself beneath Cigar's massive right shoulder, and gently lifted the tender foot between his legs. With a pair of specialized pincer-like pliers, Mott lifted the aluminum shoe from the sole of the foot, then began to scrape the sore portion of the hoof wall with a paring blade. A trickle of blood-blackened pus emerged, and with it came a measure of instant relief—both for the horse and the trainer.

Once the abscessed area on the inside of Cigar's right front foot was cut away and allowed to drain, the big horse immediately felt better. The foot was medicated to prevent infection and wrapped in cotton gauze, and for the next week Mott and his staff did little but walk Cigar around the stable and pray that the wound would heal cleanly. The Santa Anita Handicap was lost and forgotten. The date in Dubai, less than four weeks away, was very much in doubt.

To find out if Cigar could resume some sort of training, Mott had special shoes fitted to Cigar's front feet. Called "bar" shoes—so named because of the bar linking the tips of the open end of the shoe—they serve to spread the impact of the stride, thereby reducing the pressure on an injured area. On March 3, twenty-four days before the World Cup, Cigar and his bar shoes went out for a jog on the dirt course at Gulfstream Park. Jerry Bailey himself led Cigar from the barn to the track. A large crowd had gathered to witness the event. With Ralph Nicks aboard and Mott alongside on a pony, Cigar went through his paces. Back at the barn, Mott breathed a bit easier. It was a small step, but an important one.

As it turned out, Cigar did not like the bar shoes at all, and it didn't take Mott long to figure it out. Off they came, replaced by standard aluminum racing plates. It was up to the fiberglass patch applied by Jim Bayes to provide the support Cigar needed on that right front foot. Time, quite literally, was running out. Departure day for Dubai was March 16, a countdown of less than two weeks. Mott had room to give Cigar maybe two testing workouts in addition to his daily gallops, but nothing more.

On March 13, after several days of rain, Cigar was asked for more speed over a distance of six furlongs. His clocking was slow, but the muddy track was not at all conducive to fast times. On the morning of March 16, just twelve hours before Cigar's flight to Dubai, Mott had better conditions with which to work. The track was dry and freshly harrowed when Cigar, carrying Jerry Bailey, needed barely a minute and twenty-three seconds to cruise seven furlongs—faster than most competitive races at the distance. At first, the conservative Mott was a little shocked at the blistering time. But then, after Cigar had cooled down from the exercise, it all made sense. The foot was holding fast. Cigar was in a good frame of mind, acting like a horse who was ready for a race.

That night, as the lights of the Emery DC-8 disappeared in the dark Florida sky, Mott stood on the runway and lifted his hand in a salute.

"We missed a dozen days of training. He's wearing a patch. He's had just two works in the last month. And there he goes." Mott marveled at his faith in Cigar. "I guess you'd have to call that unconventional training."

It was an unconventional quest. Dubai is both a sprawling city and a sovereign state that is one of the seven United Arab Emirates. The Emirates lie near the easternmost end of the Arabian peninsula, ranging along the crescent-shaped southern coastline of the Persian (or Arabian) Gulf. The ruling Maktoum family of Dubai descended from the Al Bu Falasah branch of the Bani Yas tribe, which left Abu Dhabi in the early 1800s and headed north to settle at the mouth of Dubai Creek. Sheikh Maktoum Bin Rashid Al Maktoum, the great-great-great grandson of the original Sheikh Maktoum, rules the emirate, while his younger brothers Hamdan, Mohammed and Ahmed run various branches of the government.

Not surprisingly, they all love horses. Horse racing runs in the blood of the Arabs, for it was the Arabs who refined the fast, versatile Arabian fighting horse that was later crossed with a mixed brew of European stock to create the thoroughbred. Sheikh Mohammed, educated at Oxford, was seized early by a passion for racing. As early as 1969, when he turned twenty-one, he supervised the construction of the first racecourse in Dubai. For the next ten years, Sheikh Mohammed, his older brother Sheikh Maktoum and their friends would stage race meets, matching the best horses from their desert stables.

In 1979, Sheikh Mohammed began buying thoroughbreds on the world market. Within a few years he had assembled an international stable that was winning major races in Europe and North America. Sheikh Maktoum and Sheikh Hamdan weighed in as well, creating nothing less than a family dynasty rivaling the most successful thoroughbred stables the racing world had ever known. Few major prizes escaped their grasp. And yet, wherever he went to enjoy his thoroughbreds, Sheikh Mohammed was always the visitor, the outsider. Though comfortable in any thoroughbred setting, he longed for the day when his homeland could be recognized as a racing capital in its own right.

During the summer of 1995, Sheikh Mohammed stunned his coterie of advisors with the idea of the World Cup. He wanted to see a group of outstanding horses come to Dubai to run for a great prize and prestige. He wanted to put Dubai on display as a booming center of recreation and tourism. He wanted to preside over a great festival of sport. He wanted to be the show.

"Well, we've certainly got the name," mused Brough Scott, the veteran British racing journalist and one of Sheikh Mohammed's key advisors. "And we've got the kind of money that people take seriously. But none of that will make a bit of difference unless we get the horses. Without the best possible field we won't have the credibility. It will be like just another multi-million dollar golf tournament where only a couple of the top players bother to show up."

The World Cup needed Cigar.

Allen Paulson liked the idea. Other than bloodstock business with Sheikh Mohammed, his only encounter with Dubai had been during one of his record Gulfstream IV circumnavigations. The refueling stop at Dubai Airport had been the fastest and most efficient of the entire trip.

Surprisingly, Mott like the idea as well. After the perfect 1995 season, Cigar deserved new worlds to conquer.

"I suppose we could try to win the same races again," Mott said. "But what would it prove? If Cigar is as good a horse as we think he is, it's up to us to seriously consider a challenge like Dubai."

Mott took all possible precautions in preparing the horse for the journey. Cigar got extra nutrients, oils to lubricate his bowels and prevent intestinal compaction, and plenty of hydration en route. But in the days immediately after their arrival at the Nad Al Sheba quarantine stables, Cigar was in a funk and Jones was worried. The stables were clean, comfortable and ultra-modern, but it made no difference to Cigar, who had decided to pout until Bill Mott showed up. When he did, the big horse changed his tune. He stopped leaving grain. His coat started to glow. When he galloped, he grabbed the bit and pulled hard, just like the real Cigar.

"It's amazing," Jones said, letting his soft Arkansas drawl taste the words. "It's like Cigar knows it's time to get serious when Bill shows up. It happened in Hot Springs. It happened at Hollywood Park. And it happened here."

The international racing press assembled for Dubai—some hundred and fifty strong—swarmed Mott whenever they had the chance. What about the foot? they wondered. Would he like the track? If it continued to rain would he handle such conditions? Has he trained hard enough? What about the ban on racing medications, including the diuretic Lasix, which Cigar used where legal in America?

"Is there a worry in your mind about not being able to use Lasix here?" one journalist asked Mott.

Mott leaned forward. A mischievous grin broke through as he tapped the back of his head. "Do you see any worry?"

At that point the trainer had been in Dubai two days. Cigar was coming around.

"I'd still like to see him better tomorrow than today, and better than that the next day," Mott said as he prepared to give Cigar some exercise under the lights. "I am concerned about the track, especially if we get much more rain. I realize this is not an ideal situation for him, but we don't live in an ideal world. He has been able to meet all the challenges we've put to him. Now we'll find out if he is up to this one."

That night—it was the Sunday before the race on Wednesday—more than five hundred people gathered at Nad Al Sheba to witness workouts by not only Cigar, but several other World Cup competitors. Sheikh Mohammed, dressed in a golden robe, led his entourage to the royal viewing box as the crowd gathered at the rail and dotted the grandstand seats. Allen and Madeleine Paulson arrived, along with Dominique, as well as Oliver, Madeleine's Jack Russell terrier. Sheikh Mohammed and Oliver eyed each other warily.

"I had a dream, and now they are all here," Sheikh Mohammed proclaimed. "I am pleased that the trainers and the owners trust our facilities. If Cigar wins, he will be champion of the world. If he does not come, he can't be. I admire their courage for coming."

They came from far and wide. In addition to Cigar, American racing was represented by Soul of the Matter and L'Carriere. The British had Pentire, a top horse in his homeland, and Needle Gun, tough but in steep. Australia sent Danewin, the best colt of his generation, while Japanese racing stepped up with Lively Mount, who had won more than $4 million racing on dirt tracks.

The flag of Dubai was carried by four World Cup runners, including Halling, who had fared poorly against Cigar in the Breeders' Cup Classic, and Tamayaz, a local favorite who had run well in England. Sheikh Mohammed owned Halling, and he liked the idea of winning his own race. But he liked the idea of Cigar winning much better.

"I saw Cigar the day after he won the Breeders' Cup," Sheikh Mohammed said. "He looked like a lion. If he wins, it is the best thing for the race. If Cigar loses, he will have an excuse. I was nervous, but now I am happy. I really don't care who wins."

Race day, March 27, dawned gray and cloudy, with the ground still wet from a relentless series of storms. One week earlier, racing at Nad Al Sheba had to be canceled because of the weather. Nearly fourteen inches had already fallen in 1996 on an area whose average annual rainfall was about two inches. No one could remember such rain.

But on World Cup day, the rain stayed away. That gave the World Cup committee a better chance to complete their preparations. An expansive village with hospitality tents and booths crammed with upscale goods was set up next to the grandstand. There was a golf course winding around and inside the track, and the clubhouse served as a handsome retreat for dignitaries. A huge press tent was stocked with soft drinks, sandwiches and telephones. Bomb-trained Springer spaniels sniffed out suspicious corners, while armed military in desert camouflage patrolled the grounds.

The track had been packed tight in case of rain, yet no one was sure just how it would play.

"If it's wet, it can be a little mushy," said Richard Mandella, who trained Soul of the Matter.

"It looks a lot slower than it rides," said Mick Marshall, on hand with the Pentire crew. "I was concerned about it at first, but now I'm not."

"All I know," said Paddy Rudkin, who trained one of the top local stables, "is that I wouldn't want to be on the inside in a close finish."

The race was scheduled for seven o'clock, just after sunset. Sudanese Muslims were on their knees in traditional prayer as Cigar and the other foreign horses made their way through the crowd and into the high-walled saddling enclosure. A few minutes later the field for the World Cup emerged, looking as if they knew there was $4 million at stake.

The race was being broadcast around the world. The BBC had a crew on hand, as did America's ESPN sports network. Although no gambling was allowed in Dubai because of Islamic law, an international array of tracks and betting shops was handling millions on the race. Cigar, of course, was favored. But some of the action was downright puzzling. Broadcasting from London, commentator John McCririck could not believe what he saw.

"On the latest tote pool projection in Britain, Cigar is 7-to-4!" McCririck was positively swooning as he reported the generous price to his television audience. Cigar had been odds-on in seven straight races. "That can't last," McCririck raved on. "Americans never thought they'd live to see the day Cigar would be at odds-against in a non-handicap. If odds against Cigar was chalked up at Nad Al Sheba now, bookies would be trampled in the stampede." McCririck did not stop there. It was not just a good price on Cigar, it was a good price because of what was going to happen. McCririck lowered his voice, as if he were trying to talk a potential suicide down from a ledge. "Lots of folks don't realize," he said, "that we're about to witness from Cigar one of the most incredible performances international racing has ever seen."

Out on the track, the post parade had dispersed and Cigar was jogging around the first turn with his white shadow, Snowball, at his side. Bailey took advantage of the warm-up to get one last look at the oddly-shaped course. The World Cup, run at a mile and one-quarter, would start from a narrow chute at the southwest corner of the track. The field would run northeast for three-eighths of a mile, then make a soft left-hand turn and run due north for a bit more than a quarter of a mile before reaching a long, left-hand American-style turn that would take the field back to the southwest, toward the grandstand. Once out of the final turn, the field would be faced with a straightway grind of more than three-eighths of a mile to the finish line.

Once behind the starting barriers, Tim Jones and Snowball turned Cigar and Bailey over to the gate crew. Cigar had post number ten, with only Pentire outside him to his right. An old pro to the core, without a trace of shaky nerves, Cigar walked calmly into his starting stall, but he barely had time to square up his back feet when the starter released the doors. With a cheer from the distant stands, the Dubai World Cup was under way.

Cigar's hind legs pushed away with such force that the sandy ground slipped out from beneath his feet. As a result, Cigar found himself farther behind the leaders than usual as L'Carriere and Lively Mount led the field down the first of the three straights.

Bailey stayed cool. There was no reason to panic. Cigar quickly regained his stride and was pulling hard on Bailey's arms. After less than a hundred yards, Cigar was in a perfect spot, out from the rail, in the clear and only a few lengths behind the leaders, still L'Carriere and Lively Mount.

Bailey had spotted the green of a golf hole at the point of the first turn and was using it as a landmark. He knew, once he reached that hole, there was still seven-eighths of a mile left to run. He was determined to stay quiet on Cigar as long as he could, leaving as much energy as possible for the long final stretch.

Approaching the second turn, Bailey let Cigar have a little rein. The big horse glided up alongside the leaders, now L'Carriere and Danewin, with imperceptible ease. "The only way you know you are going faster is because you're passing horses," Bailey said. "And those horses are still running hard." As the field made its final turn, with the finish line three furlongs in the distance, Cigar was poised on the far outside, crying for Bailey to let him run. Bailey decided to wait a few seconds more.

In the meantime, Gary Stevens had methodically steered Soul of the Matter between and around horses at the back of the field. With a quarter of a mile to run, Stevens slipped past Pentire and burst from the pack, just as Bailey gave Cigar a nudge on the neck. Now, the real race had begun.

Cigar was alone in front, running hard but up to his old tricks and gearing down. Suddenly, out of the corner of his right eye, Bailey caught sight of the other horse. He thought it was some European, coming with a typical, last-minute rush. Then he saw Burt Bacharach's familiar blue silks, and the smooth, finishing power of Stevens at work, and Bailey knew exactly who it was. It was the horse his California friend, Gary Young, had told Bailey about before he left for Dubai. "This horse," Young warned, "is training out of his mind." And now Soul of the Matter was running to that training.

Bailey reached back right-handed and whapped Cigar on the rump with his whip. Cigar got the message and tried a little harder, but he shifted to his left, toward the deeper inside portion of the track. Bailey wanted him out with Soul of the Matter, where he could look his challenger in the eye.

Soul of the Matter would not be quite so easy to crack. He had run hard for a mile and one-eighth, and now he was on even terms with the best horse in the world. Cigar and Soul of the Matter were leaving the rest of the horses far behind, fighting their own private war. High up in the stands, Bacharach and his wife, Jane, were shrieking wildly for their gallant black horse. For one stride, maybe two, Soul of the Matter's nose bobbed in front of Cigar's. At the same time, though, Bailey deftly switched his whip to his left hand and tugged on the right rein. The combination angled Cigar outward, toward Soul of the Matter. Then Bailey rapped Cigar once, twice, and Cigar shot forward, as if the race had started anew.

There was still more than a hundred yards to run, but the race was at an end. Both horses were exhausted, punch drunk and wobbly, running with their heads high. Their strides had become heavy and upright. Bailey and Stevens kept driving them forward, drawing on their deepest equine pride. Through the final yards Cigar was half a body length in front of Soul of the Matter, and that is the way the race would end.

As the two horses galloped past the finish and into the shadowy clubhouse turn, Bailey patted Cigar on the neck, then reached out and slapped Stevens' extended left hand. Soul of the Matter finally trotted to a stop, well past Cigar, and Stevens allowed himself a deep, cleansing breath before coming to terms with what had just transpired. He didn't know whether to laugh or cry.

"You could say my emotions were pretty mixed," said Stevens, who was coming off the best season of his fifteen-year career. "On the one hand, you can't know what it feels like to just lose a $4-million race. But at the same time I was never in my life so proud of a horse who had just lost a race."

Soul of the Matter was led into the walking ring, along with third-place L'Carriere, and received a standing ovation of his own. Then came Cigar, and the crowd of more than twenty thousand went wild with delight.

"I thought it looked as if Cigar would be beaten," said Brough Scott, who watched the race from ground level, just past the finish line. "But what we then saw was not the Cigar of the Breeders' Cup, or the other victories. But it was a Cigar who had to dig deep, so it made it all the better.

"The real merit of the great horse is to still win when circumstances are against him," Scott went on. "And we know all the things Cigar was up against—the long trip, the foot, the sandy ground. But there you have it. The great ones come through. And the best of sport is always unscripted drama. There was Cigar, first past the winning post, under the light of a desert moon, and beating horses from all over the world and a very good horse from America."

As Cigar circled beneath the golden glow of the Nad Al Sheba grandstand and Jerry Bailey waved to the crowd, a crew quickly assembled a viewing stand for the formal trophy presentations. Sheikh Mohammed led the Paulsons and Mott through the paddock crowd and onto the track, just as Scott whisked past, herding a flock of hungry photographers into position. Sheikh Mohammed stopped and grabbed Scott by the arm. He could not disguise his joy.

"It was a dream result," said Sheikh Mohammed, his eyes bright with excitement. "A dream result."

CHAPTER 10

STREAK

The dream result of the World Cup ignited a firestorm of popularity for Cigar, even beyond the heights he already had attained as an undefeated Horse of the Year. Racing fans shared personal tales of where they were and who they were with on the day he won in Dubai, as if it were a moment to be marked in time forever. In America, the image of Paulson's patriotic colors clinging to the top of victorious Cigar stirred feelings of Olympian proportions. Not since Iroquois traveled from New York in 1881 to win the Epsom Derby had an American racehorse journeyed so far to win such a great prize.

Cigar had become a name that was suddenly hip to know. A coincidental resurgence of cigar smoking helped fan the flames. Headlines regarding Cigar became a variation on such themes ranging from "Still Smokin'" "or "No Butts About It." Sports editors who did not know a fetlock from a five iron suddenly cared about Cigar's next race. Fans lionized Cigar from stem to stern. They begged for a lock of his mane, or a few strands of his multi-colored tail. There even was a desperate woman who dove to catch Cigar's droppings before they hit the straw, defining a new and somewhat disturbing level of hero worship. Sports broadcasters began using Cigar as an example of competitive consistency in the same breath as track star Michael Johnson or Steffi Graf's domination of Wimbledon. Allen Paulson ran into Bob and Dolores Hope at a ballgame in California, and all they wanted to know about was this horse of his named Cigar. Even Brady Mott's friends at his Garden City primary school brought in news clips about Cigar and asked him for the inside story.

At a dinner in Dubai the week the World Cup was run, Brady had offered a tribute to his father. Displaying a keen insight that belied his eight years, Brady lifted his glass and said, "I'd like to make a toast to my dad, who was so brave to bring Cigar here."

Over the next five months, Mott's courage would be thoroughly tested, not to mention his ability to cope with intense public expectations. Mott once said his greatest contribution to Cigar was that he knew when to say "no" to demands placed upon the horse. As the pressure mounted, saying no would become more difficult. Not only was Cigar the idol of horse lovers everywhere, he was also looked upon by many in the racing industry as their ticket out of oblivion. By the mid-1990s, horse racing had virtually disappeared from the mainstream sports radar screen. More than a decade of declining track attendance had reduced the game to a thin niche in the recreational spectrum. Racetrack operators, desperate to survive, had begun to align themselves with casinos and slot machines. As the NBA, NFL, NASCAR and Major League Baseball secured fat television contracts, horse racing—apart from the Triple Crown and Breeders' Cup—found itself paying for the privilege of simply being seen on TV. As sports boomed in America, racing was being left behind. Cigar, the bankable star, gave the game a chance to catch up.

With Dubai in the books as his fourteenth consecutive victory, Cigar had placed his name alongside that of Man o' War on the list of significant winning streaks. Now he was within reasonable reach of the sixteen-race record established by Citation between 1948 and 1950. Such a streak was the perfect vehicle for ongoing public awareness. It provided a tangible goal, since sports fans loved a pressure-packed countdown. And the name of Citation had survived several generations with high recognition intact, providing a popular icon as a target for Cigar. Back in 1978, Pete Rose wasn't just going for the record hitting streak. He was chasing Joe DiMaggio's fifty-six in a row.

Once he returned to Belmont Park, Mott noticed that Cigar had lost a considerable amount of weight during the Dubai experience. He was not surprised. Neither was Mott overly concerned about the stressed left ankle. After a short rest, the post-race swelling never recurred. Remarkably, Cigar's injured right foot had come through the ordeal with flying colors. The Bayes patch felt tight and fresh. Mott and Paulson made no firm commitment for Cigar's next race, although the $1-million Hollywood Gold Cup on June 30 remained the next major goal.

In the meantime, the management team at Suffolk Downs was working overtime to lure Cigar to Boston for a reprise of his appearance in the 1995 Massachusetts Handicap. This time around, the stakes were higher. Cigar was not merely a popular horse on a modest winning streak. He was the best horse in the world, with his sights set squarely on a lofty, time-honored record. "If he came to Boston again, it would be the biggest thing in the history of racing in New England," said Lou Raffetto, Suffolk Downs' general manager.

In '95, Suffolk lucked into Cigar when he became eligible for the bonus that was intended to attract Holy Bull. To give Paulson enough incentive to run there again, an elaborate plan was unveiled that made Cigar eligible for a $250,000 bonus on top of the $150,000 first-place purse. Paulson and Mott still had good vibes from their previous trip to Boston. They did not need much of a push. The race fit well with the Hollywood Gold Cup, which was scheduled four weeks down the road. As the race took shape, such respectable runners as Key of Luck and Star Standard had to bow out due to injuries. Cigar was being asked to carry 130 pounds for the first time in his life, but neither Mott nor Paulson considered it an unreasonable amount, especially in the face of meager competition. On paper, the MassCap was little more than a public exhibition.

By the time Cigar was loaded onto the van the morning of May 31 for the five-hour drive to Boston, he had recovered his weight loss and then some. Cigar was walking soundly and training well, but he was also showing a thin, dark line near the back of his right front foot, a suspicious symptom that made Mott wonder if a weakness of the hoof was festering once again.

News of the slightest chink in Cigar's armor would have crushed the people at Suffolk Downs. With its tight budget and high hopes, the little track was pulling out all the stops. Cigar was being treated like visiting royalty. May 31 was declared "Cigar Day" by the Boston city council. A two-car state police escort met Cigar's van and led him down the interstate and through the new Ted Williams Tunnel. News helicopters hovered above the caravan, delivering mile-by-mile progress reports back to their television stations. Jerry Bailey would be signing autographs, with proceeds going to the injured riders fund of the Jockeys' Guild. All of Boston seemed to know that the horse named Cigar was coming to town.

Mott flew from Kennedy Airport to Boston's Logan Field, caught a cab and arrived at the track just in time to greet Cigar's van. He was not alone. More than a hundred and fifty fans, media and track officials crammed around the entry to the stable area. Every local television station was represented by a camera crew. As Mott led Cigar down the ramp of the van and into the New England sunshine, the crowd erupted into applause. Cigar looked around, as if he expected nothing less, while Mott looked down and deftly guided his horse around a pothole filled with water.

All morning long, on the day of the MassCap, visitors streamed by the barn to take a peek at Cigar. On the grandstand side, fans were pouring into the track and snapping up hats and T-shirts that screamed "The Second Coming!" For days, local television ads had been sending out the message: "If you miss the MassCap, stick around. You might see another horse this great in fifty years or so." The message was getting through.

At noon, Tim Jones borrowed a roll of yellow police line

tape and cordoned off a broad area outside Cigar's stall. "You hate to tell people no when they want to see him," Jones said. "But after awhile it just gets to be too much. The horse needs his quiet time."

Mott remained concerned about the right forefoot all afternoon. While Tina entertained family and friends in the spacious Turf Club, Bill headed back to the barn to monitor the foot. If he felt a pulse, if there was the least little bit of heat, he was ready to pull the plug. As Cigar stood in a tub of ice, the trainer talked about the calculations swirling around in his head.

"When this came up a couple days ago I had a feeling it was related to the earlier injury," Mott said. "Once a hoof is weakened by an abscess it can be susceptible to similar things down the line, just like the problem last February may have been related to the quarter crack from last fall. The thing about this one, though, is how minor it appears. I didn't want to go opening it up right on top of this race, not when it might have knocked him out for no reason at all. Chances are, whatever this is will come out whether he runs or not. The important thing is that he's comfortable today, and that we're not doing anything risky."

An hour later, Mott gave Jones the nod. It was time to tack up their warrior. A few minutes later, Cigar emerged from his stall and into a crowd lining both sides of the backstretch road. As the big bay pulled Campuzano through the gantlet, doting Cigar groupies back-pedaled in front of them, snapping quick photos with their disposable cameras. Mott followed, watching his horse, watching the crowd.

Cigar was the last of the six runners to leave the stable area and head down the stretch to the saddling paddock, just past the winner's circle. Off to Cigar's right, lining the grandstand rail, fans broke into applause as Cigar turned his head and scanned the scene. The crescendo built as the crowd thickened. They peppered both Mott and Cigar with shouts of adoration and gratitude. Mott walked alone, just behind his horse, and glanced back over his shoulder with a grin. "Isn't this great?" he asked. "They really love him."

The paddock was packed, but the Paulsons managed to squeeze through to greet Cigar as he arrived. While Mott secured the saddle, Allen was eye to eye with his horse. A group of riders clustered in the door to the jockeys' room just to get a peek at the superstar. Madeleine stood off to one side, nervously stroking the face of an outrider's pony. Once under tack and circling again, Cigar began to flex. When Bailey settled into the saddle, the juices began to flow. Cigar arched his neck and tail at the same time, as if programmed by some highly sensitive software to respond just so. "Look at him," insisted Madeleine. "That's Cigar. He knows."

The opposition, on the other hand, was unsuspecting. Among them, Cigar's five opponents had never won a major race in a hundred and eighty-six starts. Still, as Bailey noted, you've got to go around the track before they give you the money. At the start, Cigar needed an extra step to get his 130 pounds in motion. As Prolanzier and Will to Reign charged off to a quick early pace, Bailey steered wide around the first turn, then let Cigar establish his own rhythm down the backstretch. Soon, the big horse became impatient. "I didn't push any buttons," Bailey said later. "It was his idea."

Passing the half-mile marker, Cigar glided past Northern Ensign and the tiring Will to Reign, then disposed of Prolanzier as if the poor horse was nailed to the ground. With three-eighths of a mile to run, Cigar's greatest threat became boredom. Bailey let his hands move to keep the pressure on Cigar's neck. They were five in front when, from the back of the field, Personal Merit began grinding away at the deficit. Up in the stands, in the box next to the Paulsons and the Motts, owner Keith Brodkin was on his feet, screaming for his home-bred baby while the rest of the stands thundered for Cigar.

"C'mon Merit. You can do it. Get him. Get him!"

It was a delightful sight, and Brodkin was enjoying the sensation. As Bailey geared down on Cigar, Julio Pezua rode Personal Merit as if his life were on the line. Personal Merit closed the gap to an official margin of two and a quarter lengths at the end of the nine furlongs, prompting Brodkin to exclaim, "Can you imagine? Finishing that close to Cigar? I feel like we won the race."

Cigar was barely winded as he returned for the winner's circle ceremonies. The crowd pressed close to the rails and cheered at Cigar's every move. Bailey plucked a rose out of the garland and said, "It's for Suzee, if I can find her in this crowd." Lou Raffetto, wearing the smile of a man who had just delivered the goods, gazed up at his grandstand and could see most of the 22,169 in attendance. It was the largest Suffolk Downs crowd since 1966.

"I've been in the game a lot of years," Raffetto said, his voice quaking with excitement. "I was up there looking at the crowd, and I was getting chills. Look at this now!" Cigar was circling, almost taking bows. "It's like Dubai! Remember how he was out there for a half an hour? They don't want him to leave. These people aren't complacent about him at all. They know he is something very special. They might not ever see a horse like him again."

Hollywood Park management had planned its 1996 season around an appearance by Cigar. Now they would get his shot at tying Citation's record in the bargain. It was appropriate. Citation ran the final race of his career at Hollywood in 1951, winning the Gold Cup to become the first thoroughbred millionaire. Hollywood's daily programs bore Cigar's handsome image. Television and print ads whetted public appetite for his return. The Hollywood Gold Cup promised to be the most exciting race of the California season, and not only because of Cigar's presence. Waiting for him, anxious for revenge, would be Soul of the Matter and his trainer, Richard Mandella.

Then things started to go wrong. Upon returning to Belmont Park on the day after the Massachusetts Handicap, Cigar displayed some sensitivity in the right front foot. The suspicious line was generating a pulse. Bayes pulled the shoe and carved out the wounded area, then left it open to harden in preparation for another patch.

Within the week it was painfully clear Cigar would miss the Hollywood Gold Cup. He needed more time before he could be asked for strenuous exercise on the injured foot. The new bruise was at the heel, in a tricky place to repair. Bayes put his artistic skills to work and fashioned a patch that slipped down into the sole of the foot for additional support. By the time Cigar was galloping comfortably again he had lost a dozen days of training and appeared none the worse for the experience. That was of little consolation to the marketing people at Hollywood Park, who were reeling from the loss of not only Cigar, but Soul of the Matter as well. He also bruised a foot. As a gesture of support, Paulson and Mott sent the four-year-old colt Geri to California for the Gold Cup.

Geri was an understudy, but a good one. Following in Cigar's large footsteps, the son of Theatrical had won the Oaklawn Handicap earlier in the year. On the strength of a six-race winning streak, Geri was briefly nicknamed "Cigar Jr." Such talk ended when he lost the Pimlico Special. Geri finished second in the Hollywood Gold Cup, beaten a length by the Brazilian speed demon Siphon. Richard Mandella trained Siphon.

In the wake of Cigar's defection from the Hollywood Gold Cup, track owner Richard Duchossois and his staff at Arlington International Racecourse near Chicago went into overdrive. When Mott dangled the possibility that Cigar could be ready for a race on the weekend of July 13-14, the Arlington Citation Challenge jumped off the drawing board. Soon after, a backlash bubbled to the surface. Were they choosing soft spots to extend Cigar's streak? Was Paulson merely selling his horse to the highest bidder? Had they been afraid, after all, of carrying 131 pounds against California's top horses in the Hollywood Gold Cup? Paulson's reply was swift and to the point.

"How can anyone say we're ducking anything after all the places we have taken Cigar?" he wondered. "He was hurt. He couldn't run. Now he's all right and we are looking for a race. I think it is a great idea to run in Chicago. Those are great fans there. They've never seen Cigar and deserve a chance to see him run."

Any fears that the Arlington Citation Challenge would be another Suffolk Downs set-up were soon dispelled. Cigar would be carrying 130 pounds. His opposition would include Unbridled's Song, the Kentucky Derby favorite; Honour and Glory, winner of the Metropolitan Mile; Dramatic Gold, who was good enough to run third in a Breeders' Cup Classic; and Eltish, a classy English refugee in the hands of Bobby Frankel. Under the conditions of the race, Cigar would be giving them all enough weight to silence the critics. And it would be worth the trouble. With Cigar in the race, the winning horse had a chance at a first-place purse of $450,000 plus a bonus of $300,000.

With Citation's record on the ropes, the media descended upon Arlington International as if the Kentucky Derby were suddenly switched to July 13. A last-minute arrangement with CBS Sports put the Arlington Citation Challenge at the center of its Saturday sports anthology, assuring Cigar of his largest audience since the Breeders' Cup Classic the previous fall. Once again, Cigar's van from Chicago's O'Hare Field was escorted by state troopers. The racetrack invited Jimmy Jones, who trained Citation with his father, B. A. Jones, to be a special guest for the race. He praised Cigar as a fine racehorse. But no one was surprised when Jones declined to put him in the same category as Citation.

All week long, the records of Cigar and Citation were parsed and compared. Citation did his winning as a three-year-old in 1948 when he started twenty times and lost only once. His string of fifteen straight included a sweep of the Triple Crown, the American Derby at Washington Park, and the Jockey Club Gold Cup against older horses. The streak also included a walkover in the Pimlico Special and allowance wins over small fields at Washington Park and Tanforan. Citation missed the 1949 season with a variety of injuries, then came back in January of 1950 to win an allowance race at Santa Anita. The streak stopped at sixteen when he was beaten by a horse named Miche on January 26, 1950, at Santa Anita Park.

By the time he reached Arlington, Cigar's streak had gone on for more than twenty-one months. He had competed at eight different tracks in six states and one distant Middle Eastern country. Mott, the keeper of the flame, marveled daily at Cigar's resilience in the face of constant physical demands.

"All horses have bad days," he mused. "Even Cigar. All horses have bad luck in races. They get hurt. Get sick. They catch a track they can't handle. Cigar is not immune to any of these things. And yet, in spite of them all, he just keeps winning."

Mott appreciated the trip to Chicago in a different way from the other stops on Cigar's world tour. It was his old stomping grounds. He was hailed by racetrack pals he had not seen in years. "You don't forget a place like this," Mott said. There were new friends, as well. On the day before the race, eight-year-old Joey Turner appeared with his mother, Sue Martinez, at Cigar's barn and presented Mott with a T-shirt he had made. On the shirt was an imprint of a photo from *People* magazine, showing Mott holding a cigar in his teeth and the horse at his side.

On the morning of the race, Gerard Guenther, Cigar's lanky exercise rider, had his hands full as the big horse pulled his way around the large, nine-furlong Arlington oval. For a moment, on the far turn, Cigar was lost in the glare of the sparkling summer morning. "There he is," Tim Jones said, pointing in the direction of the three-eighths pole. "I can see his silver tail with the sunlight glistening through it." The horse was driving everyone to poetic heights.

The scene in the paddock before the Challenge felt more like a prize fight than a horse race. Every time the packed crowd caught a glimpse of Cigar a fresh roar went up. Some of the other horses were startled—most noticeably Unbridled's Song. But Cigar fed on the noise. With each new cheer he arched his neck a little tighter and pranced a little quicker. As the field left the paddock and walked through the tunnel to the track, the booming echo of one last cheer bounced off the walls and sent Cigar into a double-time that had Jones and Campuzano hanging on for dear life.

Once on the track, Mott took Cigar by the bridle and escorted him into the clear before turning him over to the escort pony. The roars continued from the 34,223 in the stands. "I wasn't worried about Cigar," Mott said as he made his way to his seat. "It was the pony who was losing it. I wanted to make sure he had calmed down before I let go."

Just before arriving at his seat, Mott spotted Joey Turner and his mother in the crowd. "Have you got a place to sit?" They didn't. "Joey, you come with me."

Out on the track, Cigar was standing stone still on the backstretch, sniffing the breeze and looking for airplanes. Bailey loved the way he was acting. Warming up, Cigar had slipped into one of his fancy dressage dance steps, switching his back lead foot with every stride. He was pulling out all the stops. When the field approached the gate and the din hit college football decibels, Cigar stopped again, cocked his head in acknowledgment, and walked into the outside post position of the starting gate without so much as a second thought.

Then the race was on. As expected, Honour and Glory jumped out to the early lead. Behind him, Mike Smith kept Unbridled's Song off the pace and glued to the side of Cigar. As a result, Cigar took the first turn at least six lanes wide. Up in the stands, Mott felt his stomach churn. "That was exactly what I was worried might happen," he said.

Cigar continued to race on the outside down the backstretch, while Honour and Glory came under pressure from Dramatic Gold. Unbridled's Song faded quickly, giving Cigar a chance to shave a little off the far turn before ranging up alongside Dramatic Gold. His rider, Corey Nakatani, caught sight of Cigar and let his horse corner wide into the stretch, leaving Cigar far out in the middle of the track once again. Jerry Bailey was hot.

"I don't mind if a jock is race-riding," Bailey said of Nakatani's move. "We all do that. What I don't like is when they don't do it right. If you're going to float me wide, then as soon as you straighten into the stretch you drop down and take advantage of what you've done. Instead of that, Nakatani kept on packing me out. It made no sense."

Dramatic Gold was running the race of his life, but it was not enough. With a furlong to run, Cigar cracked the spirit of his rival and began to ease clear. Up in the stands, a dazed Joey Turner stood in front of Bill Mott as the people around him went mad. As Cigar flashed under the finish line three and a half lengths in front of Dramatic Gold, Sue Martinez looked over at her son, with his Chicago Bulls cap backwards on his head, and smiled at the sight. "He's going to be a big deal at school this week, that's for sure," she said.

Cigar had reached number sixteen, and the Chicago fans went wild. For nearly twenty minutes they stood and cheered. While Mott, Paulson and Bailey were interviewed for TV, Cigar circled out on the track and the rest of the party—including Joey Turner—assembled on the turf course for photographs. As Bailey remounted and the volume increased, a track attendant draped a garland of flowers across Cigar's withers. Mott glanced down at the yellow ribbons trailing a bit too close to Cigar's feet. With Cigar on the move, Mott bent over and tied up the ribbons with a quick half hitch, getting them safely out of the way.

"When he stops," Bailey warned to the assembled photographers, "you'll have about four seconds to shoot." Cameras exploded. One, two, three, four. Bailey pulled a carnation from the garland, tossed it to Suzee, and jumped to the ground. The Paulson party headed for their helicopters in the infield and hopped directly to a nearby private runway, where Allen's Gulfstream IV was warmed up and waiting to take them to a cancer research fund-raiser honoring Paulson that night in Los Angeles.

A little while later, as the Gulfstream zipped just north of Paulson's hometown of Clinton, Iowa, the man who owned Cigar gave up the controls and tried to unwind from the incredible day.

"It's a dream to breed a horse like Cigar and watch him race," Paulson said as he sank into one of the Gulfstream's deep, leather passenger seats. "But then to see how the fans come out and cheer for him. I never thought I'd ever see anything like it. I'm glad we took him to Chicago. How many people do you suppose will be at Del Mar when he goes for the record? I'd imagine they've never seen anything like what's going to happen when he shows up there."

Cigar would try to topple Citation in the $1-million Pacific Classic at Del Mar on August 10. He prepared for the race at Saratoga Springs, where Mott leased the storied Greentree Estates training facility owned by the family of John Hay Whitney. Greentree was, quite literally, through the looking glass—a fairyland of expansive vistas, towering pines, a private training track, and two barns with airy wooden stalls.

"This is really roughing it," Mott liked to tell his visitors as he spread his arm and fanned across the green panorama. "This is where thoroughbreds were meant to be trained."

While Del Mar braced for an unprecedented onslaught of fans, media and attention, Cigar bounced back from his Chicago effort and fell into a comfortable routine at Greentree. Mott scheduled his final breeze for August 7, the day before they were scheduled to leave New York for the assault on Citation. Cigar responded with an efficient six-furlong workout before an estimated four to five thousand fans. Among them was Alex Hassinger.

"It will always be a great memory," said Hassinger, who had left his position with Paulson in early 1995 to form his own public stable. "He was just as I remembered him. Bailey was on him with his hands set in a cross on his withers. The reins were very, very loose. Cigar walked straight for the gap, and Bailey never moved. Twenty yards from where you actually walk onto the racetrack there were maybe two hundred people surrounding the gap. He stopped, by himself, turned his head all the way to the left and looked, then turned his head all the way to the right and looked. After a couple minutes just standing there he walked onto the track and turned left. Bailey never moved."

The field awaiting Cigar in California had a familiar feel. There was Soul of the Matter, who had not run since Dubai; Dramatic Gold, still fresh from his effort in Chicago; and Tinners Way, who had won the last two runnings of the Pacific Classic. Between them they were zero-for-five against Cigar. The fresh meat included Siphon, Luthier Fever and Dare and Go. Richard Mandella, Mott's counterpart in the West, had three of the contenders.

And then there were two. The black cloud following Soul of the Matter descended once and for all on the Wednesday before the Classic when he strained a ligament in a workout. The injury ended his career, leaving behind the burning image of his race against Cigar in the desert.

Cigar arrived the following day and was bedded down in the Bill Shoemaker barn, just to the east of Del Mar's new, mission-style grandstand. Friends and family made the pilgrimage as well, anxious to be a part of history. Don Mott, who managed a helicopter fire and rescue service in the San Francisco Bay Area, brought his wife and three sons south to watch Cigar in action for the first time. Rob Mott came in from Mobridge with a South Dakota delegation that included Ray Goehring and his wife, Lenora, and Steve Krumm, the man who watched over Bill Mott's recently purchased herd of fifty-two Angus cows.

"We charge fifty dollars just to let people drive by and look at Bill Mott cattle," Krumm said. "It's a lot more if they stop."

Early on the morning of the Pacific Classic, five of the six horses in the field took to the track for their final gallops. They were all alone. The general horse population, some twenty-five hundred strong, was kept behind the barriers until Cigar, Tinners Way, Dramatic Gold, Siphon and Dare and Go finished their exercise. Cigar pulled Guenther hard down the back-stretch and around the turn. Almost too hard, as far as Mott was concerned. Down on the ramp Ray Goehring called

Lenora's attention to Dare and Go, a compact son of Alydar, straining hard as he went through his paces for Mandella.

"Look how he's almost getting away from the boy," Goehring said. "That horse is wanting to do something."

When Del Mar opened its gates at nine o'clock on the morning of August 10, fans began filling the stands as never before. The previous record crowd was 34,697, set on opening day of the 1994 season. More than two hundred representatives of the media were on hand, putting the resort town track on the map as never before in its sixty-year history. By the time the Classic was run, the fans numbered more than forty-four thousand strong.

It seemed as if all of them tried to cram their way into Del Mar's amphitheater paddock to see Cigar. They were not as raucous as the Chicago fans, or as affectionate as the Boston crowd. But when Bailey mounted up and Cigar began to prance, a bolt of pure electric excitement sent thousands of voices to screaming his name. Some kind of history was about to be made.

Cigar's sleek coat leaked a layer of sweat as he completed his warmups and fell into the final procession to the starting gate, located at the extreme west end of the track. For some reason, Cigar balked when he was led to his starting stall. Bailey tapped his rump and the assistant starters gave the big horse an insistent tug before Cigar would load. To his left the Mandella horses stood waiting for the bell: Siphon, poised to take the lead, and Dare and Go, a horse who had not won a major race for a year and a half.

Siphon shot to the front immediately, but Bailey was ready. He gave Cigar enough urging to stay just behind the leader as the field whisked past the teeming stands and into the clubhouse turn. After conferring with Mott, Bailey was convinced he needed to keep Siphon in his sights, lest he steal away to a slow pace and retain more strength for the finish, as he did in the Hollywood Gold Cup against Geri. Cigar was game for the try, although he was not pulling as hard as he had on Bailey's hands in races as recent as Dubai and the Donn.

Siphon and Cigar were joined down the backstretch by Dramatic Gold, and the pace picked up considerably. On the far turn, with three furlongs to run, Dramatic Gold was finished. Cigar pulled alongside Siphon, and Siphon said goodbye. So far, the race was following the predictable Cigar script. Citation was the only horse left for him to pass.

Then, as Cigar rounded the final bend, Dare and Go began gaining ground. Was it another illusion? Was this Personal Merit again, coming along for a noble second at Suffolk? The answer was a chilling no. Dare and Go meant business, and suddenly Cigar appeared vulnerable. Bailey drew the whip and gave the big horse a crack, but out in the middle of the track it was Dare and Go with all the momentum. His rider, Alex Solis, pushed Dare and Go past Cigar as fast as possible to open a daylight lead. Cigar tried for a few strides to respond, but on this day there would be no answer—no deep reserve from which to draw, as he had found in the desert of Dubai. As Bailey folded his hands and let Cigar wind down, Dare and Go crossed the finish line three and a half lengths in front. The streak was over.

It was over. The Paulsons and the Motts stood in their box and stared into the distance, concerned more for their horse than the results of the race. When Cigar returned intact, beaten for the first time in almost two years, the crowd hailed him with a grateful ovation. Dare and Go received polite applause and a smattering of boos. Both Mandella and Mott fought their way through the crowd to track level, one floating on air, the other in a daze.

For the next two hours, as the Classic was dissected to bits, Mott was asked, over and over, to explain the inexplicable. He was patient at first, citing the fast pace and the pressure from Dramatic Gold. He wondered himself why Cigar had balked at the starting gate. And he was openly critical of his own strategy that sent Cigar chasing after Siphon at all costs. After awhile, Mott's answers grew weary. He would start a sentence and then trail off, hoping the rest could be filled in later.

"You know, sometimes they just get beat," Mott said. "The expectations for Cigar are incredibly high. I mean, for a long time he was able to overcome all the things that get even the best horses beat: injuries, Mother Nature, racing luck, all those things. It would have been nice to have set the record. But seeing Cigar's name up there alongside Citation...well, there's nothing wrong with that. He's still Cigar as far as I'm concerned."

Watching Mott from afar, Richard Mandella could not help thinking back to the night of March 27 when Cigar broke his heart and beat Soul of the Matter in Dubai. It was a good feeling, at long last, to slip the shoe onto the other foot, even though Mandella's admiration for Cigar and Mott knew no bounds. "Cigar is a great horse," he said. "The winning streak has been good for everybody. And Mott is unshakable. He's smart. He's a good sport, and a fierce, fierce competitor. But after Dubai, this feels awful good. I don't think I'll ever get over that race. But this sure helps."

Late in the day the Cigar crew gathered back at the Shoemaker barn to watch the big horse unwind. Cigar was subdued, almost moody, as Tim Jones led him around the ring. "He looks so sad," said Madeleine. Her daughter Dominique thought she knew what to do, and unwrapped Cigar's favorite treat, a peppermint. As Cigar made a pass she held out her hand, figuring he would gobble up the candy and forget about his troubles. Cigar stopped, sniffed at the offering, and then turned away. Mott's jaw dropped like a rock.

"I don't believe I saw that," Mott said. "He's never turned one of those down in his life."

Jim Bayes picked up on it right away. "He's mad at himself, getting beat by that pan-footed son of Alydar. He's just plain embarrassed."

Cigar turned down two more peppermints that afternoon before finally accepting one, and then another. His people lingered late at his stall, reluctant to leave. The fluorescent lights overhead cast a stark, merciless glare on the scene. The Paulsons, the Motts and the Baileys shared a few consoling words, but they did not need to say much. They were all veterans of a hard game. They knew that, in the scheme of things, victory and glory were the exception to the rule, and that Cigar's incredible streak had been the greatest exception of them all.

"I feel bad for the fans," Allen Paulson said. "They're the ones who came here to see him win."

"But after all Cigar has given us," Madeleine Paulson added, "how can we possibly complain? We can only be grateful. Besides, now that the streak has ended I can go back to wearing colors again! Since it started, I've been afraid to change from anything other than variations of black and white."

Back at the Motts' Saratoga house, Brady had watched the race unfold with growing horror. "No, no, no!" he screamed as Cigar gave way to Dare and Go.

"I was so depressed," Brady admitted. "I didn't talk for like an hour after the race. My dad called me that night and we talked about it. He said there's a first time for everything, and things like that just have to happen sometimes. I still love Cigar."

In the end, it was Ray Goehring, Mott's mentor and friend and a horseman to the core, who provided the best parable of winning and losing—and living to fight again another day.

"We had an old horse named Ben Bo," Goehring said as he sifted back through the years. "Ran him nineteen times and he won eighteen at the country fairs. Then one time we matched him against a little horse named Honest Abe, for three hundred dollars. For South Dakota, that was a lot of money. At that time we had a little cafe and beer parlor in Herreid.

Before the race I told the guy that ran my place to fill the cooler with beer. I took one look at that little pigeon-toed horse we were running against and I knew we were gonna beat him.

"I had my cousin ride my horse. The other guys had a professional jockey, and we got outfoxed. To this day I think they bought the starter off. Every time our horse would break, this old-time jockey would just grab his horse and holler, 'No go! No go!' Before my kid could get our horse stopped he'd run about four blocks. They did that three times before they finally said go. We got beat a head.

"That was a pretty good education," Goehring sighed. "After the race I called the guy running our cafe to shut the cooler and raise the price."

EPILOGUE

The end of the streak did not mean the end of Cigar. Far from it. In defeat Cigar received an outpouring of public support reserved only for the most cherished heroes. The Internet buzzed with sentimental e-mail. Trade magazines were swamped with faxes and letters. And while the Paulsons opened sympathy cards and notes of consolation, Richard Mandella got hate mail.

"I had a lot of people come up to me," Bill Mott said in the days following the race. "Some of them I know didn't really like me. But they were all very kind. After awhile, I got the feeling the race hit his fans pretty hard. Maybe even harder than those of us closest to the horse. After all, they only knew him as a racehorse in the afternoon. And every time they saw him he won. Every day I went to work, I still got to spend time with Cigar. Win or lose, he could never let us down."

The streak was but a number. Cigar was made of flesh and blood. For one brief moment, in the crucible of the Pacific Classic, he proved to be vulnerable. Sometimes Emmitt Smith could be held to less than a hundred yards. Sometimes Ken Griffey Jr. went 0-for-4 at the plate. And sometimes Greg Norman missed the cut. On this rare occasion Cigar lost a race. Perhaps it was the pace. Perhaps it was the strategy. Or perhaps it was some mysterious internal timeclock that chose August 10, 1996, to give the real Cigar the afternoon off.

Viewing from a distance of three thousand miles, John Nerud watched the race and knew it was not Cigar's day.

"Knew it the second he wouldn't load in the gate," said the training legend. "Horse does that, he's trying to tell you there's something not quite right. Now I guess people will wonder if he was the greatest after all. That was never important to me. There's no way you can compare horses from different eras. The question is not whether Cigar is the greatest in history. The fact is, he's become a part of history."

Cigar continued to make headlines as well as history. A Japanese breeder offered Paulson $30 million for the horse. Paulson was impressed, but he turned down the deal. "I would miss him," Paulson said. Cigar rewarded Paulson's decision by winning the Woodward Stakes at Belmont Park on September 14, his first race after the Pacific Classic. As the hard-core New York fans pressed forward and screamed their undying devotion, Mott pumped his fist in the air and Bailey took Cigar on a victory trot up the stretch. Paulson, standing off to the side, wiped a tear from his eye.

After the Woodward, there were only two races left for Cigar before his likely retirement: the Jockey Club Gold Cup at Belmont and the Breeders' Cup Classic at Woodbine in Toronto, Canada. Mott knew his time with Cigar was running out. A chapter of his life would be at an end. "I'm not sure just how long it will take for me to truly appreciate what a great horse he is," the trainer said. "I suppose I will after I've gone a long, long time without one nearly as good."

If racing history teaches anything, it would be a long, long time before anyone found a horse nearly as good as Cigar. Or as popular. Or as full of personality and pride. It figured to be a long, long time before there would be another horse who could bring people out on cold, damp mornings just to watch him gallop. Or pack the stands in every corner of the racing world. Or inspire tears and chills as he reached out with a stride that took no prisoners.

On the morning of the 1996 Massachusetts Handicap, a little girl, maybe seven or eight years old, braided her golden pigtails with ribbons of red, white and blue. It was a special day, because her father was taking her to Suffolk Downs to meet her thoroughbred hero. When the time came they stood near the rail, and the little girl jumped up on her father's shoulders for a better view. Then suddenly, at the end of a long procession, there he was, larger than life and looking her straight in the eye. The little girl smiled and waved and yelled loud enough for the horse to hear:

"I love you, Mr. Cigar!"

ABOUT
THE AUTHOR

Jay Hovdey began writing about thoroughbred racing in the mid-1970s and can't seem to stop. His work has appeared in magazines and journals around the world, from New Zealand, Australia and Japan to Canada and the United Kingdom. In America, he has written for *Reader's Digest,* the Los Angeles *Times* and the New York *Times,* in addition to such racing publications as *Daily Racing Form, The Racing Times, Thoroughbred Record, Thoroughbred Times, Spur, Equus* and *The Thoroughbred of California.* Since 1992, Hovdey has been the California correspondent for *The Blood-Horse* magazine, North America's leading thoroughbred weekly.

Hovdey is the author of two other books, including *Whittingham: The Story of a Thoroughbred Racing Legend,* published in 1993 by The Blood-Horse, Inc.

Along the way Hovdey has collected two Eclipse Awards for magazine writing, the David F. Woods Award for coverage of the Preakness Stakes, and the Joe Hirsch Award for coverage of the Breeders' Cup. In 1995 he was honored by his peers in the National Turf Writers' Association with the Walter Haight Award for career excellence in turf writing.

Hovdey is a second generation Californian, foaled the same year as Dark Star, and lives with his son in Laguna Niguel.

Past Performances

CIGAR'S RACES 1993-96

Owner	Jockey	Trainer
Allen E. Paulson		William I. Mott

White, Red Yoke and Emblem, Blue Sleeves, White Stars, Blue Cap

Cigar — **Jerry Bailey**

B.h.6 Palace Music-Solar Slew by Seattle Slew, MD

1996:	5	4	1	0	$3,930,000	Turf:	11	1	2	4	$82,015
1995:	10	10	0	0	$4,819,800	Off:	2	1	0	0	$1,560,000
Life:	30	18	3	4	$9,019,815						

10Aug96	Dmr6	1¼		ft	$:45^{96}$	$1:33^{66}$	$1:59^{85}$	3u	PacifcClG1-1500k	4/6	2^{1}	$2^{½}$	1^{1}	$2^{½}$	$2^{3½}$	Bailey,J	124	BL	*.10	DmdGo^{3½} Cgr^{7} Sphn(BRZ)^{8}	stalkd fst pce,2ndbest
13Jul96	AP10	1⅛		ft	$:46^{90}$	$1:10^{28}$	$1:48^{30}$	3u	ApCitation-1075k	10/10	$6^{3½}$	$6^{2¾}$	3^{1}	$1^{½}$	$1^{3½}$	Bailey,J	130	L	*.30	Cgr^{3½} DrmtcGld^{nk} Eltsh^{2}	lost ground drew clear
1Jun96	Suf10	1⅛		ft	$:45^{82}$	$1:10^{30}$	$1:49^{63}$	3u	MassH-500k	3/6	4^{6}	3^{3}	1^{3}	$1^{4½}$	$1^{2¼}$	Bailey,J	130	BL	*.10	Cgar^{2¼} PrsonalMerit^{10¼} Prlanzier^{nk}	handily
27Mar96	Uae	*1¼		gd			$2:03^{84}$	4u	DubiWrldCp 4000000	11	---	---	---	---	$1^{½}$	BaileyJ	125			Cigar^{½} SouloftheMatter^{8} L'Carriere^{¾}	
10Feb96	GP10	1⅛		ft	$:46^{90}$	$1:10^{96}$	$1:49^{12}$	3u	DonnHG1-300k	1/8	$3^{1½}$	3^{2}	2^{hd}	$1^{2½}$	1^{2}	Bailey,J	128	L	*.20	Cgr^{2} WkvSprngs^{4} HvnlyPrze^{3}	rated, easily
28Oct95	Bel8	1¼		my	$:48^{35}$	$1:35^{67}$	$1:59^{58}$	3u	BCClasscG1-3050k	10/11	3^{1}	$4^{¾}$	$1^{1½}$	1^{2}	$1^{2½}$	Bailey,J	126	L	*.70	Cgr^{2½} L'Crre^{1} UgcntdFr^{¾}	took over 4w trn,drvng
7Oct95	Bel10	1¼		ft	$:48^{06}$	$1:36^{12}$	$2:01^{29}$	3u	JkyClbGCG1-869k	6/7	3^{1}	2^{1}	2^{1}	$1^{1½}$	1^{1}	Bailey,J	126	L	*.35	Cgr^{1} UncntdFr^{9¾} StrStndrd^{2}	stalked outs,clear
16Sep95	Bel9	1⅛		ft	$:45^{80}$	$1:09^{66}$	$1:47^{07}$	3u	WoodwardG1-596k	5/6	$3^{2½}$	3^{4}	2^{hd}	1^{4}	$1^{2¾}$	Bailey,J	126	L	*.10	Cgr^{2¾} StrStndrd^{3} GldnLrch^{¾}	cruised in hand
2Jul95	Hol6	1¼		ft	$:45^{69}$	$1:34^{01}$	$1:59^{46}$	3u	HolGCupHG1-1000k	1/8	4^{2}	$4^{1½}$	1^{1}	1^{3}	$1^{3½}$	Bailey,J	126	BL	*.90	Cgr^{3½} TnrsWy^{hd} Tsfthcn^{½}	much best, driving
3Jun95	Suf10	1⅛		ft	$:47^{20}$	$1:10^{54}$	$1:48^{74}$	3u	MassH-750k	6/6	$3^{3½}$	$3^{1½}$	$2^{½}$	1^{3}	1^{4}	Bailey,J	124	BL	*.20	Cgr^{4} PrBtHnst^{5½} DblClvds^{nk}	4 wide, ridden out
13May95	Pim10	1 3/16		ft	$:48^{16}$	$1:11^{56}$	$1:53^{72}$	4u	PimSpecHG1-600k	1/6	$1^{1½}$	1^{1}	$1^{1½}$	$1^{4½}$	$1^{2¼}$	Bailey,J	122	L	*.40	Cgr^{2¼} DvlHsDue^{2¾} Cncrn^{4½}	steady hand drive
15Apr95	OP9	1⅛		ft	$:46^{44}$	$1:10^{90}$	$1:47^{22}$	4u	OaklawnHG1-750k	4/7	$4^{2½}$	$4^{5½}$	4^{2}	1^{hd}	$1^{2½}$	Bailey,J	120	L	*1.70	Cgr^{2½} SlvrGbln^{4} Cncrn^{1}	rallied, drew clear
5Mar95	GP9	1¼		ft	$:47^{55}$	$1:36^{96}$	$2:02^{95}$	3u	GulfstmHG1-500k	9/11	$4^{3½}$	$4^{3½}$	3^{nk}	1^{4}	$1^{7½}$	Bailey,J	118	L	*.50	Cgr^{7½} PrdfBrkn^{1} MhgnyHl^{2}	as rider pleased
11Feb95	GP9	1⅛		ft	$:46^{48}$	$1:10^{76}$	$1:49^{68}$	3u	DonnHG1-300k	4/9	1^{1}	1^{2}	1^{hd}	$1^{½}$	$1^{5½}$	Bailey,J	115	L	4.00	Cgr^{5½} PrmtvHl^{2} BnsMny(GB)^{3½}	dueled, drew off
22Jan95	GP10	1 1/16		ft	$:46^{82}$	$1:11^{45}$	$1:43^{22}$	4u	Alw34400nw4/x	5/8	1^{hd}	$1^{½}$	1^{1}	1^{1}	1^{2}	Bailey,J	122	L	*.50	Cgr^{2} UpngthAnte^{8¾} ChsnGld^{1}	led throughout
26Nov94	Aqu8	1		ft	$:45^{98}$	$1:11^{21}$	$1:36^{10}$	3u	NYRAMiHG1-250k	6/12	$4^{1¼}$	4^{1}	1^{2}	1^{5}	1^{7}	Bailey,J	111		8.90	Cgr^{7} DvlHsDe^{2½} PnchLne^{1}	drew off, rddn out
28Oct94	Aqu6	1		ft	$:44^{76}$	$1:09^{85}$	$1:35^{78}$	3u	Alw34000nw2/x	6/6	2^{hd}	$1^{1½}$	1^{3}	1^{4}	1^{8}	Smith,M	117		3.50	Cgr^{8} GldnPlover^{3½} Glviegold^{2}	ridden out
7Oct94	Bel8	1 1/16	Ⓣ	fm	$:46^{65}$	$1:10^{87}$	$1:41^{40}$	3u	Alw36000nw3/x	2/6	$4^{2½}$	$3^{3½}$	2^{hd}	3^{3}	$3^{8½}$	Krone,J	117		3.40	UncntdFr^{2½} SmOldWsh^{6} Cgr^{½}	mid move, 4 wide turn
16Sep94	Bel7	1	Ⓣ	fm	$:45^{52}$	$1:08^{66}$	$1:33^{14}$	3u	Alw34000nw2/x	10/11	$8^{4¾}$	$7^{3¾}$	4^{6}	$6^{5½}$	$7^{8¼}$	Bailey,J	117		*1.90	Jdo^{2½} BrmdCdr^{2} LmtdWr^{2}	wide all, no threat
8Aug94	Sar1	1⅛	Ⓣ	fm	$:47^{58}$	$1:12^{02}$	$1:48^{61}$	3u	Alw34000nw3/x	1/8	$4^{2½}$	4^{3}	$4^{1½}$	$4^{1¼}$	3^{3}	Smith,M	117		3.20	MyMgl^{1½} NxtEndvr^{1½} Cgr^{nk}	in tight, steadied
8Jul94	Bel7	1 1/16	Ⓣ	fm	$:48^{52}$	$1:12^{63}$	$1:43^{07}$	3u	Alw34000nw3/x	5/5	2^{hd}	1^{hd}	2^{hd}	$4^{1¼}$	4^{9}	Smith,M	117		*1.70	DncngHntr^{½} Cmpdre^{3} I'mVryIrsh^{5½}	dueled, tired turn
20Nov93	Hol6	1⅛	Ⓣ	fm	$:46^{28}$	$1:10^{44}$	$1:46^{88}$	3	HolDerbyG1-400k	9/14	$5^{2½}$	$5^{4½}$	$4^{1½}$	$7^{6½}$	$11^{14¼}$	Valenzuela,P	122	BL	24.80	ExplsvRd^{1¼} JnHme^{nk} ErlfBrkng(IRE)^{½}	bid turn, gave way
5Nov93	SA8	1⅛	Ⓣ	fm	$:48^{11}$	$1:12^{33}$	$1:48^{03}$	3	VolanteHG3-111k	4/9	4^{4}	$4^{2½}$	3^{2}	$2^{1½}$	2^{2}	Valenzuela,P	117	BL	7.70	EstrnMmrs(IRE)^{2} Cgr^{nk} SnkEys^{½}	finished well
25Sep93	BM5	1 1/16	Ⓣ	fm	$:45^{74}$	$1:10^{04}$	$1:41^{66}$	3	AscotHG3-100k	1/11	$5^{3¾}$	$5^{4¾}$	$4^{1½}$	$1^{3½}$	3^{nk}	Valenzuela,P	117	BL	4.10	Sbe^{nk} Nnprdctvst^{hd} Cgr^{2¼}	room rail, led, wknd
3Sep93	Dmr8	1	Ⓣ	fm	$:47^{01}$	$1:11^{10}$	$1:35^{06}$	3u	Alw40000nw3/L	4/6	2^{2}	2^{2}	2^{1}	2^{hd}	$2^{½}$	McCarron,C	115	BL	3.30	KngdmfSpn^{½} Cgr^{½} Strnno^{3}	bid 1/8,outfinished
18Aug93	Dmr5	1 1/16	Ⓣ	fm	$:47^{40}$	$1:11^{21}$	$1:41^{81}$	3u	Alw36000nw1$/x	5/10	$4^{3½}$	$4^{3½}$	$5^{3½}$	1^{hd}	$1^{2¾}$	McCarron,C	115	BL	*1.90	Cgr^{2¾} OrMtnGmtd^{hd} ThBrklyMn^{2¼}	quick gain early str
12Jun93	Hol10	1 1/16	Ⓣ	fm	$:48^{00}$	$1:11^{61}$	$1:41^{46}$	3	Alw39000nw2/L	10/10	7^{5}	$7^{2½}$	$4^{¾}$	$3^{1½}$	$3^{1¾}$	Valenzuela,P	117	L	2.90	Nnprdctvst^{½} Tsfthcn^{1¼} Cgr^{2¾}	in tight 1/4,rallied
23May93	Hol9	1 1/16	Ⓣ	fm	$:47^{25}$	$1:10^{75}$	$1:41^{38}$	3	Alw39000nw1$/x	11/12	3^{2}	3^{1}	2^{hd}	$1^{1½}$	$4^{1¾}$	Valenzuela,P	117	BL	3.80	Plsdntxpln^{½} SttlyWrrr^{½} FltWzrd^{¾}	lead 1/8, faltered
9May93	Hol3	6f		ft	$:22^{19}$	$:44^{73}$	$1:09^{56}$	3u	Msw	3/6	4	2^{1}	1^{hd}	1^{2}	$1^{2¼}$	Valenzuela,P	117		5.20	Cgr^{2¼} GldnSlwpy^{5½} FmsFn^{hd}	off slowly, rushed
21Feb93	SA6	6f		gd	$:21^{92}$	$:45^{48}$	$1:10^{91}$	3	Msw	9/9	7	6^{4}	$7^{5¾}$	6^{7}	7^{13}	Valenzuela,P	118	B	5.10	Demigod^{nk} Cardiac^{2} SirHutch^{2½}	no factor

PEDIGREE
FAMILY NOTES

CIGAR
b h, April 18, 1990

PALACE MUSIC, ch, 1981	The Minstrel, 1974, 9s, SW, $570,762, 510 f, 58 SW, 2.45 AEI	Northern Dancer, 1961, 18s, SW, $580,647, 635 f, 146 SW, 5.14 AEI	Nearctic
			Natalma
		Fleur, 1964, 22s, wnr, $9,235, 9 f, 7 r, 5 w, 4 SW	Victoria Park
			Flaming Page
	Come My Prince, 1972 Unraced 8 f, 8 r, 6 w, 1 SW	Prince John, 1953, 9s, SW, $212,818, 553 f, 55 SW, 2.42 AEI	Princequillo
			Not Afraid
		Come Hither Look, 1962, 23s, SW, $28,727, 14 f, 12 r, 12 w, 1 SW	Turn-to
			Mumtaz
SOLAR SLEW, dkb/br, 1982	Seattle Slew, 1974, 17s, SW, $1,208,726, 622 f, 73 SW, 4.89 AEI	Bold Reasoning, 1968, 12s, SW, $189,564, 61 f, 10 SW, 3.75 AEI	Boldnesian
			Reason to Earn
		My Charmer, 1969, 32s, SW, $34,133, 12 f, 8 r, 6 w, 4 SW	Poker
			Fair Charmer
	Gold Sun, 1974, 48s, SW, $161,492, 9 f, 8 r, 6 w, 1 SW	Solazo, 1959, 78s, SW, $140,532	Beau Max
			Solar System II
		Jungle Queen, 1956, 8s, wnr, $1,593, 11 f, 9 r, 9 w, 5 SW	Claro
			Agrippine

CIGAR'S RACE AND (STAKES) RECORD
(through August 10, 1996)

Year	Age	Sts	1st	2nd	3rd	Earned
1993	at 3 in NA	9	2	2(1)	2(1)	$89,175
1994	at 4 in NA	6	2(1)	0	2	$180,840
1995	at 5 in NA	10	10(9)	0	0	$4,819,800
1996	at 6 in NA, UAE	5	4(4)	1(1)	0	$3,930,000
Lifetime		30	18(14)	3(2)	4(1)	$9,019,815

Sire: PALACE MUSIC, ch, 1981. Standing 1996 breeding seasons in Japan and Australia. Raced 3 yrs in Eng, Fr, and NA, 21 sts, 7 wins, $918,700. Won John Henry H (gr. IT), Dubai Champion S (Eng-I), Bay Meadows H (gr. IIT), La Coupe de Maisons-Laffitte (Fr-III), Prix Daphnis (Fr-III), Col. F. W. Koester H (T); 2nd Breeders' Cup Mile (gr. IT), Prix Jacques Le Marois (Fr-I), Inglewood H (gr. IIIT), La Coupe de Maisons-Laffitte (Fr-III), Prix Messidor (Fr-III); 3rd Washington, D.C., International (gr. IT), Dubai Champion S (Eng-I), Hill Rise H (T).

Lifetime: 6 crops, 185 North American foals, 110 rnrs (59%), 82 wnrs (44%), 22 2yo wnrs (12%), 16 sw (9%), 3.24 AEI, 1.68 CI, 43 sale yrlgs, avg $15,897, 0.5 TNA.

In 1996: 3 sw, 0 2yos, 0 2yo rnrs, 0 2yo wnrs.

1st dam: Solar Slew, dkb/br, 1982. Bred by Carl J. Maggio and Murty Farm (Ky.). Raced 1 yr, 7 sts, 0 wins, $5,856. Dam of 7 named foals, 3 rnrs, 3 wnrs, 2 sw. Sent to Arg 1990. Returned to NA 1995. ($335,000, 1983 kenjul yrlg; $510,000, 1984 ctbmar 2yo).

1987: Forli's Slew, b f, by Forli (Arg). Unraced. Sent to Arg 1990. Returned to NA 1995.

1988: MULCA, dkb/br f, by Raised Socially. Raced 2 yrs in PR, 38 sts, 15 wins, $189,542. Champion imported 3yo filly in PR. Won Clasico Roberto Clemente (PR-II), Clasico Prensa Hipica (PR-II); 2nd Clasico Accion de Gracias (PR-II), Clasico Roberto Clemente (PR-II), Clasico Eduardo Cautino Insua (PR-III). ($11,500 ftmmay 2yo). Died 1992.

1989: Strawberry McSlew, dkb/br c, by Strawberry Road (Aust). Unraced.

1990: CIGAR, b c, by Palace Music.

    At 3: 2nd Volante H (gr. IIIT); 3rd Ascot H (gr. IIIT).

    At 4: Won NYRA Mile H (gr. I).

    At 5: Horse of the Year, champion older male. Won Breeders' Cup Classic (gr. I), Hollywood Gold Cup H (gr. I), Jockey Club Gold Cup (gr. I), Oaklawn H (gr. I), Pimlico Special H (gr. I), Gulfstream Park H (gr. I), Woodward S (gr. I), Donn H (gr. I), Massachusetts H.

    At 6: Won Donn H (gr. I), Dubai World Cup, Arlington Citation Challenge S, Massachusetts H; 2nd Pacific Classic (gr. I).

1991: Corridora Slew (Arg), b f, by Corridor Key. Raced 2 yrs in Arg and NA, 10 sts, 4 wins, $35,014.

1992: Soltin, dkb/br c, by Cautin.

1993: Barren.

1994: Potriprince (Arg), dkb/br c, by Potrillazo. Unraced.

Broodmare sire: SEATTLE SLEW, dkb/br, 1974. Sire of 180 dams of 599 foals, 393 rnrs (66%), 287 wnrs (48%), 96 2yo wnrs (16%), 2.62 AEI, 2.23 CI; 42 sw here and abroad.

2nd dam: GOLD SUN, b, 1974. Bred by Haras La Quebrada (Arg.). Raced 5 yrs in Arg and NA, 48 sts, 14 wins, $161,492. Won Gran Premio Internacional Ciudad de Buenos Aires (Arg-I), Clasico Francia (Arg-III), Clasico Wilfredo Latham (Arg-III), Clasico Guillermo Paats (Arg-III), Clasico Estados Unidos de America (Arg-III), Clasico Ecuador, Clasico Francisco Narciso de Laprida, Clasico Peru; 2nd Clasico Eliseo Ramirez (Arg-II), Clasico Coronel Pringles (Arg-II), Clasico Aniversario de la Loteria de Bene Nacional y Casinos (Arg-III), Clasico Republica Federativa del Brasil (Arg-III), Clasico Arenales (Arg-III), Clasico General Francisco B. Bosch (Arg-III), Clasico Adolfo y Rufino Luro; 3rd Gran Premio Internacional Ciudad de la Plata (Arg-I), Clasico Primera Junta de Gobierno (Arg-III), Clasico Jorge Atucha (Arg-III), Clasico Republica Federativa del Brasil (Arg-III), Clasico Ecuador. Dam of **JUNGLE GOLD** (f, Master Willie; $147,251, Won Locust Grove H; 2nd May Hill E.B.F. Stakes, Eng-III; 3rd Goffs Irish One Thousand Guineas, Ire-I, Del Mar Oaks, gr. IIIT), **Seattle Sunrise** (c, Seattle Slew; $47,927, 3rd Fappiano H).

3rd dam: Jungle Queen, b, 1956. Bred by Hernan Ceriani Cernadas. Winner at 3 in Arg. Dam of **JUNGLE DUCHESS** (f, Make Tracks; Champion 2yo filly in Arg, Won Clasico Gilberto Lerena, Clasico Cotejo de Pontracas - Jorge de Atucha, Clasico Carlos Casares, Clasico Saturnino J. Unzue, Gran Premio Seleccion; 2nd Clasico Criadores, Clasico Miguel Angel Y Tomas Juarez Celman; 3rd Clasico Arturo R. Bullrich, Argentine One Thousand Guineas, Clasico Circulo de Propietarios de Caballerizas Sangre Pura de Carrera, Clasico Polla de Potrancas, Clasico Eliseo Ramirez, Gran Premio 25 de Mayo; producer), **SUNNY DAY** (f, Solazo; Won Clasico Maipu, Arg-II, Clasico Espana, Arg-III, Clasico Comando Y Direccion General de Remonta Y Veterinaria, Arg-III, Clasico Direccion Provincial de Hipodromos, Arg-III, Clasico San Luis, Arg-III, Clasico Guillermo Paats, Arg-III, Clasico Saturnino J. Unzue, Arg-III, Clasico General Francisco B. Bosch, Arg-III, Clasico Primer Paso; 2nd Clasico General Alvear; 3rd Clasico Eliseo Ramirez, Arg-II, Clasico Jockey Club de Montevideo, Arg-III; producer), **SUNNY SUMMER** (c, Solazo; Won Clasico Tratado Antartico, Clasico La Cascada, Clasico Escuela Granaderos de San Martin, Clasico Sociedad Rural Argentina; 3rd Gran Premio Suipacha, Arg-I, Clasico Rio Parana, Clasico Congreso de Tucuman), **MATRERO** (c, Make Tracks; Won Clasico Club Estudiantes de La Plata-Campeon de America, Clasico Nigromante), **Jungle Mythologic** (f, Mount Athos; 2nd Clasico Colombia, Arg-III; dam of **SALT SPRING, Juvenilia**). Granddam of **JEWELLERY, JUNGLE COUNTESS**. Family of **DUDDLE BUG MEL, RARE HOSTAGE, AFRICA MIA, JAZZMAN, JUST IN CASE, JET SELLER, TRAVEL TALK**.

ACKNOWLEDGMENTS

A book would have been impossible without the cooperation and enthusiasm of the people who were touched by the power of Cigar's personality. Of course, he would have preferred a bucket of peppermints.

Three strong couples deserve most of the credit. They deferred to Cigar at every turn, yet they willingly shared their own stories, not to mention their personal photographs. It is not an exaggeration to declare that without Allen and Madeleine Paulson there would be no Cigar. The author owes them his gratitude, just as horse racing can never repay them for breeding and campaigning their star. Bill Mott took care of Cigar and Tina Mott took care of Bill—it is impossible to imagine one without the other. Jerry and Suzee Bailey provided a lesson of grace and style in a dangerous game.

Cigar's extended family included Ted and Mac Carr and the staff of Brookside Farm North, Laura and Emmanuel de Seroux, Lee Ricci, Alex Hassinger, and Steve Allday, as well as Josh and Ellen Pons and the crew at Country Life. Bill Mott surrounded himself with class acts, from his brothers, Don and Rob, to Jim Prendergast, Ray Goehring, Tim Jones, Ralph and Judy Nicks, Simon Bray, Tom and Fonda Albertrani, Juan Campuzano, Dave Wallace, Gerard Guenther and the incomparable Jim Bayes. Thanks also to Bill Nack, Chick Lang and Brough Scott, for their penetrating thoughts, and to Richard Mandella, for making Cigar run hard.

Just as Cigar was always a collaboration of talent, so was this book. Brian Turner led the design team, with aide from Suzanne Depp and Jeff Burkhart. Diane Viert provided valuable research, and together with Pat Dolan and Debbie Tuska gave the text quality control. Patricia Lankford and Anne Eberhardt distilled the work of Barbara Livingston and a host of fine photographers, with help from Janet Pieren and the Paulson archives in California. Finally, Ray Paulick and Stacy Bearse—trusted editor and loyal publisher—must take their bows for making this book come true. *— The author*